M000239667

The GOD-Centered Homeschool

GCH PUBLICATIONS
744 Burton St
Rocky Mount, NC 27803

© 2017 by Justin C. Nale

All rights reserved. No part of this book may be reproduced in any form without permission in writing from the publisher, except in the case of brief quotations embodied in critical articles or reviews.

All Scripture quotations, unless otherwise noted, are from the ESV® Bible (The Holy Bible, English Standard Version®), copyright © 2001 by Crossway, a publishing ministry of Good News Publishers, 2011 Text Edition. Used by permission. All rights reserved.

Printed in the United States of America.

For Crystal

Contents

1)

Why God-Centered?

---

*"Whatever you do, in word or deed, do everything in
the name of the Lord Jesus, giving thanks to God
the Father through him."*
- Colossians 3:17

Imagine a group of Christian parents talking together in someone's living room. Perhaps these are fellow church members in a small group meeting, conversing after the "official" meeting has ended. The question comes up: What do you want most for your kids?

One parent answers very honestly. "I want my kids to be *happy*." Most of the others nod their heads in agreement. Isn't this what all parents want for their children?

Another parent, however, a bit proud that he has a more spiritual answer, says, "I want my kids to be *holy*." The others think about this. Slowly, they begin to concede to themselves that holiness ought to be their goal for their children. Still, they don't feel as eager about pursuing their children's *holiness* as they did their *happiness*.

A third parent, sure that he has an answer to trump the others, says in his most reverent and dignified tone, "What I want most is for God to be glorified in my children. Whatever their lot may prove to be, if He is glorified, I will be content."

What do you think about these three answers? What should parents want most for their children? What do you want most for *your* children?

If we are Christians, we know that we must affirm the last answer. God's glory must come before the happiness or even the holiness of our children. If we place our children above God and His glory, we turn them into idols and imperil not only our souls but theirs. God's glory is the umbrella under which all of our other desires and motives must find their place. *"So, whether you eat or drink, or whatever you do, do all to the glory of God"* (1st Corinthians 10:31).

The Three Goals are One

One of the most wonderful truths of Scripture for Christian parents is that we do not have to choose between the three answers given above. The reason we do not have to choose is that all three of these purposes go hand in hand. In fact, in the great work of parenting, these three goals are actually *one*.

Let's take for starters the goal of *happiness*. When parents speak of wanting their children to be happy, they certainly do not mean a glib, superficial, flimsy kind of happiness. What they mean is that they want their children to have a deeply-rooted, unshakable, all-consuming, unending joy. Isn't this what we want for our kids? *True* happiness? This kind of happiness can only be found in God. He is the fountain of living waters (Jeremiah 2:13), the altogether desirable One (Song of Solomon 5:16), the God of glory (Psalm 29:3) and of beauty (Psalm 27:4). In His presence there is fullness of joy, and at His right hand are pleasures forevermore (Psalm 16:11). Therefore, Christian parents who truly have the happiness of their children as their goal will do all they can to help those children know and enjoy *God*.

But what about *holiness*? Surely the holiness of our children must be a higher priority to us than their happiness. After all, God tells us explicitly to be holy as He is holy (1 Peter 1:16). There is no verse that explicitly tells us to be *happy* as He is *happy*.[1]

The breakthrough comes with the astonishing realization that holiness consists in finding one's total happiness in God. This is why seeing God is the fitting reward for the pure in heart; He is the one thing they want most of all (Matthew 5:8). To be holy, or pure, is to have a heart so centered on God that there is no impulse left in the soul to forsake Him. The heart fully satisfied in Jesus has no capacity to be compelled towards evil, but will say as Joseph did, "How can I sin against my God?" (Genesis 39:9). Moreover, the heart which is drawing up overflowing buckets of delight from the fountain of God's glory will never hesitate to obey any command God gives, but will say, "*I delight to do your will, O my God*" (Psalm 40:8). Indeed, greater delight will be found in the obedience. This is why heaven will be a place of eternal happiness in God *and* a place of eternal holiness. One is the root, and the other is the fruit. The path to holiness is joy in God.

Why is this so helpful to homeschooling families? It helps us to see that the education of our children is *not* disconnected from the discipleship of our children. When we can help our children see and rejoice in the glory of God in each subject they study, we are also helping them grow in faith, holiness and Christian maturity. A God-centered education aims at the happiness of our children *in God* in every subject for the sake of their holiness.

God Glorified in the God-Centered Joy of Our Children
What about that third goal, the one which trumps all others? What about the desire that God be glorified in our children? It must be said here that many Christian parents have known the sadness of children who never came to know the Lord. In their youth and adulthood, these children continually rejected the gospel appeals of their parents, and chose to live lives of rebellion against God. This fatal choice meant that these children would never know true happiness or true holiness. Yet it has been a comfort to some Christian parents, and rightly so, that though their children chose to reject Christ, God would still be glorified. When we truly love our Creator and have hearts centered on Him, we can find some measure of peace even in the tragic case of lost children, knowing that ultimately even their lives and destinies will magnify the greatness of our God.

That said, we can also joyfully affirm that Christian parents should not fulfill their parental responsibilities in fear, but in the prayerful, hopeful trust that if we train up our children in the way they should go, when they are older they will not depart from it (Proverbs 22:6). The working assumption is that our children will glorify God as vessels of His *mercy,* not as vessels of His *wrath* (Romans 9:21-24). This means that the desire for God to be glorified in our children can be fully united with our desire that our children be saved and find full enjoyment in Christ.

John Piper has said that "God is most glorified in us when we are most satisfied in Him."[2] God is seen most accurately as the great and wonderful Being that He is when His people reflect to the world in attitude, words, and actions that He is more valuable to them than anything else. This means that the happiness of our children in God not only leads to their holiness, but also to their lives serving as a witness to the greatness and grandeur of God. Aiming for God's highest glory in our children's lives and aiming for their highest satisfaction are in fact

11

the same aim. God is most glorified in our children's education when that education leads them to be most satisfied in Him.

This, then, is the true aim of Christian parenting: that our children would know and enjoy God. Everything we do for our children should find its place within that noble mission

Education as Part of God-Centered Parenting

This is not a book about parenting, but homeschooling. Nevertheless, we must not miss the connection between the two. I am making an argument here. If the true aim of Christian *parenting* is that our children know and enjoy God, then the true aim of our children's *education* must also be the same. Why?

First, it should be noted that Scripture places the education of children under the broader calling of parenting. Children have been entrusted by God to their parents, and education is one of the primary ways that parents are to fulfill their sacred trust. This does not imply that all or even most of a child's education must come directly from his parents, but it does imply that parents are responsible before God for doing what they can to ensure their children have the best education possible. This responsibility does not lie mainly with professional educators or with society as a whole. We do our children a great disservice when we divorce education from parenting and disconnect the goals aimed at in each endeavor. It is not professional teaching groups or government officials who should establish the goals of our children's education, but parents as they consider each child holistically, with education serving as one major facet of the overall discipleship of their children.

Second, related to what has just been said, we must recognize that children are whole beings. Their brains are not disconnected from their hearts or their wills. The education they receive will do more than simply store facts in their minds. It will play a role in shaping their opinions and attitudes, their beliefs and convictions, their worldview, and ultimately, their character. Many people can testify how their lives were shaped and their future paths were decided by something they learned in a classroom! Therefore, we must not isolate the education of our children from our broader goals of seeing them grow to be godly men and women. If the goal of Christian parenting is that our children know God and enjoy God, this must also be the ultimate goal of our children's education.

A Personal Concern

Over the last ten years, I have had the wonderful experience of interacting with hundreds of homeschooling parents. In one role, God even gave me the opportunity to ask several hundred homeschooling moms (and the occasional dad) in one-on-one interviews about their homeschooling journeys and their reasons for choosing home education. These conversations were often rich and encouraging. They opened my eyes to gracious work that God is doing in the lives of families all over the United States and Canada.

One not-so-surprising discovery that I made during those conversations is that the vast majority of Christian homeschoolers choose home education for reasons of *faith*. Sometimes homeschooling was chosen in order to remove the children from ungodly peer influence in public or private schools. Other times the choice was made because of disagreement with liberal agendas or anti-Christian teaching in classrooms. For some parents, the opportunity to give their children a Christian education was just too good to pass up. What all of these parents desired is that their children receive an education consistent with biblical principles and Christian character.

How are these homeschooling families doing on reaching this aim? The results seem decidedly mixed. There are some positive steps that many Christian families are taking. Many choose to include a Bible curriculum as part of the scope of their children's education. They are careful to choose a "Christian" curriculum for certain subjects, especially science. Alongside the standard secular literature that would be found in most schools (Shakespeare, Hawthorne, Dickens), Christian homeschool parents often have their children reading. C. S. Lewis and Tolkien, as well as biographies of Christian heroes and missionaries. This is all good.

Yet my sense is that most students are having very few worshipful moments during their typical homeschool day. Even with Christian curriculum, our students are far too seldom finding their hearts well up in awe towards God as they learn. Explicit connections to God are few and far between in the material and in our students' minds. Greater *happiness* in God is seldom an actual practical result of the day's

13

educational activities. Though most Christian parents would agree that we should homeschool for the purpose of helping our children know and enjoy God, there seems to be a disconnect between our stated desire and our actual practice.

This is the disconnect that I pray this book will help remedy. It does not offer a full solution, but only advice from a homeschool father who has tried to think deeply about this issue for the sake of his own family and others. God gripped me some years ago with a desire to help Christian homeschoolers grow in becoming more *authentically* God-centered. I have found that it is all too easy to talk about being God-centered in the abstract, and much more difficult to actually put that talk into practice. It is the *practice* of God-centered homeschooling that this book is about.

What Lies Ahead
Perhaps it will help to survey the landscape ahead. In chapter two I will share some marks of a God-centered homeschool. These marks are not the *main* thing I have to say, but they are important reminders. Without these marks, even the best approaches and methods to educating our children will fall flat. That chapter is a call for our homeschools to be truly *Christian*. The end of the chapter offers some helps for us as we pursue these marks.

In chapter three I will try and describe the approach to God-centered homeschooling that I call "the God Grid". This grid flows out of my experience with one verse of the Bible that crashed upon my thinking some years ago. That verse took hold of me and would not let me go. It seeped into my bloodstream and began to open doors of thought that had previously been closed. That verse provides for us the God Grid that we can place upon any subject matter, always pointing us back to God in at least three ways. This grid is certainly not the only way to be God-centered in our homeschooling, but it is one approach that my family has found helpful, and it has been an encouragement to others as well. I will seek to illustrate the God Grid in that chapter.

In chapters four through seven I will attempt to give further help in using the God Grid by applying it to various subjects. Math is a subject that parents often struggle to turn in a Godward direction for their children, so we will discuss that in chapter four. In the fifth chapter we will look at science, and how to help our students move from an understanding of scientific principles to adoration of the God who established those principles. In chapter six we will turn to language and literature, applying the God Grid to fictional stories. Finally, in chapter seven, we will focus on history and give advice on how to help our children see God's sovereign hand in the turning of history's pages.

Two Ditches to Avoid
"We educate our children for Heaven, not Harvard." This a statement that I have heard (and repeated to others) many times over the last decade. Rightly understood, it is a *good* sentiment. Though it is sobering to consider, we are not promised that our children will make it to adulthood. What we do know is that one day our children will stand before the Judgment Seat of Christ, and that they will have to give an account. What will matter on that day is whether our children have come to know God and love Him. Because eternity is more important than the here-and-now, and because this life is only a vapor which is here today and gone tomorrow, the faith and character of our children must be more important to us as parents than their ability to multiply numbers or diagram sentences. Those abilities are important as well, but they pale in comparison to the importance of faith. If our children receive an education that enables them to gain much knowledge and many skills, but does not lead them to love Jesus Christ, then we have missed the mark that matters most.

There are two ditches we must avoid. The first is *intellectualism*. This is the error of focusing on our children's minds as disconnected from their hearts. In intellectualism, we are concerned only with how much our children know and understand. Have they memorized important facts? Can they regurgitate them when called upon? Do they understand Newton's Laws of Motion? Can they find Istanbul on a map? Can they write a properly sourced research paper?

Let me be clear: knowledge is good! The Proverbs teach us over and again that it is fools who despise knowledge. Since all truth is God's truth, it is right and noble to seek to learn and understand as much truth as possible. Let us teach our children to be earnest in the pursuit of knowledge!

But the Proverbs also teach us that knowledge puffs up. If knowledge is not accompanied by the fear of God, it will lead us into arrogance. Too many homeschool students have far-excelled their peers in academics, but are cocky and rude and demeaning towards others. If we are to protect our children against the pride that knowledge can bring, we cannot focus only on their minds. We must focus also on their hearts. We must work to ensure that the facts they learn have their proper *humbling* effect – and this happens only when God is seen in relation to those facts. When we behold God in a subject, we cannot be puffed up. We see ourselves as small compared to Him. Or greater still, we don't see ourselves at all, because His glory in that subject has gained our full attention and adoration.

The other ditch that we must avoid is the ditch of *emotionalism*. This is the mistake we make as parents when we aim for the hearts of our children while *bypassing* their minds. Rather than helping them see God in every fact, we ignore the facts and just keep insisting to our kids that God is awesome and they should love Him. This proves to be of little help to our kids, because God has not called us to an empty sentimentality, but to a love for Him based on *revelation*. That is, God has revealed Himself in this world, in truth, in facts, and it is through seeing Him in those truths that our hearts are stirred to love and worship.

In every subject, the goal is to combine mind and heart together. We want our students to think deeply and love warmly. We want them to experience many "lightbulb" moments as ideas click in their minds, but then through those moments we want them to see the God behind all true wisdom and understanding. Head and heart together – that is our approach.

Beware the "Get-It-Done" Mentality
Before I close out this first chapter, I want to make you aware of one great obstacle to God-centered homeschooling. It is the "get-it-done" mentality. It is a mentality that I confess I struggle with too often. I love checklists. I love the feeling of crossing off items on my to-do lists and watching the list shrink throughout the day as various jobs get done. Productivity by itself can be very fulfilling.

In homeschooling, however, this mentality causes all sorts of problems. Mom becomes more concerned with helping her children make it through the day's assignments, and less concerned with the actual learning itself. Once our children are older and more independent, we are often more likely to ask them about their progress in completing assignments than actually discussing the content of those assignments. In the upper high school years especially, many students are robbed of the opportunity for a truly life-changing, character-shaping educational experience in order to focus on checking off boxes and making sure the appropriate credits have been attained for college.

This get-it-done mentality is especially disruptive to a God-centered education, because seeing and savoring God in every subject requires *time*. It cannot be rushed. The glory is found in thinking upon the subjects at hand and how they relate to God. If we replace this goal with the goal of simply finishing assignments, we are short-circuiting the ultimate purpose of education. We are substituting pragmatic efficiency for soul-shaping experiences with the Almighty. Throughout the homeschool years, whether we are working with younger elementary students or upper high school students, we must keep this command in mind: *"Be still and know that I am God"* (Psalm 46:10).

In the formation of our children, we do them a greater service if we help them learn less, but more deeply, than if we help them learn more, but only superficially. Or to put it differently, it is better for our students to learn less material, but to understand it well and see God's glory in that content, than for them to learn much more information without seeing God at all. What is the ultimate purpose of education? It is to help our children know and enjoy God.

A Prayer

Father, thank You for the children You have entrusted to my care. They are a precious gift from Your hands. Thank You for Your promise that in Jesus Christ You will supply my every need as I seek to parent and educate my children for Your glory. I praise You for Your boundless mercy, and the fountain of forgiveness from which I must drink every day.

O God, help me to keep the proper priorities in my homeschooling. Help me to guide my children in seeing Your glory in every subject. Protect me from the temptation to care more about the assignments being accomplished than You being seen and savored by my children.

Help me to make much of You before their eyes, and open their eyes, that they may come to know and love You with all their hearts.

In Jesus' Name, Amen.

2)

Marks of a God-Centered Homeschool

---

*"But he said to me, 'My grace is sufficient for you, for
my power is made perfect in weakness.' Therefore I
will boast all the more gladly of my weaknesses, so that
the power of Christ may rest upon me."*
- 2nd Corinthians 12:9

Homeschooling is not for the faint of heart. It is an adventure, and like all adventures, it requires courage.

Some of the obstacles that we face on the journey can be foreseen. We know there will be days when our best-laid plans for our children will be interrupted by sickness. Wiping noses and caring for aching bodies will take priority, and homeschooling will need to take a back seat. Sometimes, it will be us who are sick, and our children may find themselves on an unplanned school break.

We know that we will constantly run up against the sin in our children's lives. There will be many moments when their stubbornness or anger or laziness will show itself. Children do not come out of the womb submissive, eager to listen and learn, ready to work hard for Jesus. In their early years, an assignment completed without complaining might be a victory in itself. Once our children hit puberty and begin to enter young adulthood, sinful tendencies that we may have thought were conquered often reappear again, with new vigor.

Along the journey, we can expect that there will be seasons of weariness. No calling, no matter how high and wonderful, remains exciting all of the time. Many homeschool parents experience the springtime itch, a phenomenon I have noticed around March of each year in which homeschool families suddenly become tired of what they have been doing and start looking for alternatives. One homeschool resource store in our area says that March is their best month for sales because so many families want a change in curriculum when spring comes around.

Weariness can also build over years of homeschooling. Many moms who excitedly began homeschooling their children when they were only four or five years old find that they have almost completely checked out once their children reach high school. These latter years are the *cream* years, the years in which we can have the greatest impact on the kind of adults our children will become, and engage them in the most wonderful conversations. Weariness is an obstacle we should expect to face in that leg of the homeschool journey, and we should resolve to persevere. Finishing well is vital.

Alongside these and many other foreseeable obstacles are those that we cannot foresee. In the last year alone, I have seen several homeschooling families that we love have their lives put on hold by a cancer diagnosis, a death in the family, an unexpected move, and even a failed marriage. When we begin this adventure, we must admit that we simply do not know all that lies on the path ahead. Only God knows.

I've reserved the most important obstacle for last. The greatest enemy of our homeschools is the sin in our own lives. It is our own impatience, anger, and selfishness that have the potential of doing the most harm. When our hearts are cold towards God, how can we teach our children to rejoice in Him? When we find ourselves doing the very things we've taught our children not to do, how can we instruct them with integrity? Children can sniff hypocrisy from a mile away. It is so easy for us to get caught up in the circumstances and trials of our lives, and to take our own eyes off of God. Too often we allow ourselves to become so busy with a thousand different activities that we fail to be still and know that He is God. Our prayer lives begin to shrivel. Our church attendance becomes sporadic. Our hearts feel a diminishing hunger for God's Word.

When we consider the great calling we are attempting to fulfill – to help our children know and enjoy God in every subject – and then consider our own sinfulness and weakness, we might well begin to despair. Surely we are only setting ourselves and our children up for failure. But when we find ourselves on our faces before God, acknowledging that the job is too hard for us, we are precisely where God would have us be! We do not glorify God by homeschooling in our own strength, but depending on the strength that He provides. *"But we have this treasure in jars of clay, to show that the surpassing power belongs to God and not to us."* Our insufficiency is the stage on which God displays His faithfulness.

Our desire should never be to deceive people into thinking we have it all together. This temptation can be strong when we are surrounded by other families who seem to have homeschooling all figured out. The children are always well-behaved, eager to learn, and excel at every subject. Their mother is always well-kept, full of joy, soft-spoken, and overflowing with encouragement toward others. Their home operates like a finely tuned machine, without any quarreling or conflicts. As far as we can tell, *their* homeschool has never experienced a bad day.

Yet this is not reality. As a pastor, I have discovered through personal experience that the homeschool families many of us admire from the outside and believe match the description above are actually as fallen and in need of grace as the rest of us. While all of us should aim for well-behaved children and peaceful homes, we need to be open and honest with everyone that we homeschool as recovering sin-addicts, looking every day to God's grace to be our strength. God is most glorified in our homeschool when it is clearest to ourselves, our children, and the world that we are weak, but *He* is strong.

Faith

This means that one central mark of the God-centered homeschool is *faith*. We look to God and not ourselves for success in our homeschooling. We rest in His great love. We hope in His promises.

The benefits of educating our children out of a heart secure in God's love cannot be understated. In Romans 8:35 Paul asks, *"Who shall separate us from the love of Christ? Shall tribulation, or distress, or persecution, or famine, or nakedness, or danger, or sword?"* Paul then provides the glorious answer to this question in verses 38-39: *"For I am sure that neither death nor life, nor angels nor rulers, nor things present nor things to come, nor powers, nor height nor depth, nor anything else in all creation, will be able to separate us from the love of God in Christ Jesus our Lord."*

This means that once we have come to believe in Jesus Christ, we can be sure that we will live in God's great love forever. This love is not fickle and it does not fade. This love does not depend upon our behavior or our faithfulness, but on Christ who is the same yesterday, today, and forever. In the midst of whatever obstacles we face, God's love is a refuge for our souls; a fortress, a constant source of security, confidence, and peace. The simple truth that many of us learned as children remains profound and life-giving: *Jesus loves me, this I know, for the Bible tells me so.* By faith, we take hold of this glorious truth and live in it.

The promises of God are an expression of His love to us. Just like an automobile runs on gasoline, our homeschools should run on God's promises. In a car, the engine processes the fuel and converts it into motion so that the car is propelled forward. In our lives, our hearts of faith are the engine, and the promises of God are the fuel. As we trust God's promises, take them to heart, and look forward to their fulfillment, they are transformed into power to propel us forward in obedience. We find divine energy – a strength that is not our own – as we believe that God hears our every prayer (1st John 5:14), that He will never leave us nor forsake us (Hebrews 13:5), that He is working all for our good (Romans 8:28), and that the sufferings of today are not worth comparing to the glories ahead for us (Romans 8:18). As parents and teachers, we find the power for God-centered homeschooling in believing these precious promises.

Prayer

A second mark of a God-centered homeschool is *prayer*. Prayer is faith in action. We express our dependence upon God by praising and thanking Him for His faithfulness, and bringing before Him our present needs and concerns. If we trust God little, we will pray little. If we truly believe that He is able and willing to do great things for our families, we will pray much.

A great motivator to prayer is the realization that our greatest desires for our children cannot be achieved by us, but only by God. It does not matter how well we love our kids, model Christ to them, or educate them - if God does not open their eyes to His glory and grant them repentance and faith, they will never know or enjoy Him. "*By grace you have been saved through faith. And this is not your own doing; it is the gift of God*" (Ephesians 2:8). All of the character goals that we have for our children, as well as their ability to truly see and savor God in each subject, depends entirely upon His blessing our efforts and making them effective. Therefore, nothing is more important in our homeschooling than making sure that we are seeking God's face. We must persevere in interceding for our children, asking God to turn our schooldays into worshipful experiences. There is much more for us to do after we pray, but nothing that should take priority over prayer itself.

We must make time for prayer. We know from experience that certain appointments in our lives take priority over others. A scheduled play-date with another family must be postponed when a significant doctor's appointment falls on the same day and time. Similarly, we must cultivate the habit of prioritizing our daily communion with God above our other obligations. We must dismiss the notion that our busyness is the key to success, for God can do more for our children in one second than we can do in a thousand years of homeschooling. Martin Luther famously said, "Too busy to pray? I am too busy not to pray!"

We must pray with earnestness. The Puritans used to speak of "wrestling with God" in prayer, lifting up their concerns and reminding God of His promises until they received a sense of assurance in their hearts that they had been heard. When we are interceding for our children, or bringing our anxieties or doubts or questions about our homeschooling before God, we should pray from the heart, with eagerness. Charles Spurgeon said, "Prayer pulls the rope below, and the great bell rings above in the ears of God. Some scarcely stir the bell, for they pray so languidly; others give but an occasional pluck at the rope; but he who wins with heaven is the man who grasps the rope boldly and pulls continuously, with all his might."[3]

What are we to pray for concerning our homeschooling? Certainly we should pray for the conversion of our children. Nothing is more important than this. We become far too easily concerned with more temporal matters to the neglect of eternal matters, and sometimes we forget to pray for what is most important. If we truly desire our children's happiness, here is the way for them to be eternally happy: they must come to trust in Jesus. We should not stop praying for saving faith in the hearts of our children until we are sure that our prayer has been answered. We should be like hunting dogs that do not give up the chase until they have caught their prey. We should be like the persistent widow that continued to pester the judge until her request was granted. Until God has answered, let us never stop shooting heaven with arrows of prayer for the salvation of our children. *"Continue steadfastly in prayer"* (Colossians 4:2).

Related to this, we must pray regularly for our children's joy in God. We should lift up the various subjects that our children will be studying, the books they will be reading, the conversations we will be having with them, and the assignments they will be completing. We should ask God to bless each of these so they will serve to deepen the wonder and esteem our kids have for God. Our desire should be for God to give our children an eagle-eye for His glory everywhere they look.

We must pray also for our children's growth in maturity. Farmers in a field may plant seeds and keep them watered, but it is only God who can give the growth. So also, as we plant seeds in the hearts of our children and seek to water them through God-centered teaching, we know it is God alone who can bring about true Christian maturity in our children. In this regard, we should keep in mind Christ's precious promise in Matthew 7:7: *"Ask, and it will be given to you; seek, and you will find; knock, and it will be opened to you."* Our God is not reluctant to give grace to our children. He is eager. Our responsibility is to be persistent and earnest in asking for this grace, so that when it is given He will get the glory.

One important aspect of our children's maturity that might be an appropriate subject of special prayer is their work ethic. Followers of Jesus are to be marked by their diligence, and we should long for our children to become hard-working, industrious men and women. This is a life-skill that we should seek to cultivate in them while they are still very young. *"Whatever you do, work heartily, as for the Lord and not for men, knowing that from the Lord you will receive the inheritance as your reward. You are serving the Lord Christ"* (Colossians 3:23-24). Many parents can testify to the frustrations that can occur when a child refuses to do his work, or refuses to do it well. Yet the wills of our children spring from their hearts, and these are in the hands of the Lord. He can do what we cannot – incline the hearts of our children so that they desire to be diligent. This grace for our children is worthy of our heartiest prayers.

Of course, we should also pray *with* our children. At the beginning of each new day, we can teach our children to live by faith as we instill in them the habit of seeking God's blessing before approaching any task. Through prayer we can join with our children in asking that God would reveal more of Himself to them, and that He would give them the proper attitude and strength to learn what He would have them learn.

Few practices model the life of faith for our children better than the simple act of beginning each day together in prayer.

Scripture
A third mark of the God-centered homeschool is *Scripture*. We have already discussed how Scripture serves as an encouragement to our homeschooling, feeding our faith with glorious truths and precious promises. Here I want to unpack the role of Scripture as a *worldview lens* for our homeschools.

All of us interpret the world around us and the new information we receive each day through our preconceived notions. These notions determine how we understand reality. For example, one person may read that the Appalachian Mountains are more than 300 million years old and scoff, because his preconceived notions do not allow for an earth that old. Another may read the same information and embrace it as truth, because his worldview allows for such possibilities. Both are encountering the same information, but reject or embrace that information based on their worldview lens.

Everyone has a worldview, including our youngest children. Our worldview is not static, but dynamic, constantly being molded and refined. Before we come to Christ, our worldview is egocentric, focused on ourselves. Our lens is tinted by our own selfish desires and thoughts. When we are born again, a Copernican Revolution begins to take place in our mind and heart, and Christ increasingly becomes the center of our understanding of reality. We die to ourselves and begin to find greater joy in seeing the world as all about Christ. "*In Christ are hidden all the treasures of wisdom and knowledge*" (Colossians 2:3). The more Christ-centered our worldview becomes, the closer we get to seeing the world accurately, as it really is. "*The fear of the LORD is the beginning of wisdom; all those who practice it have a good understanding. His praise endures forever!*" (Psalm 111:10).

As Christians, we believe that God has spoken through His Word, the Bible. Therefore, when we use the teaching of the Bible to mold and refine our worldview, we can be sure we are seeing the world accurately. This is one of the great benefits of our faith: while most people's worldviews remain fickle because they are based on the changing opinions of men, a Christian's worldview becomes increasingly stable as it rests on the unchanging foundation of God

Himself. God does not change, His Word does not change, so the Christian worldview is sturdy and strong.

God has not only revealed Himself in the pages of the Bible, but also in creation. The Bible and the physical world are the two great books God has given to mankind that we may know Him. The revelation of God in the Bible is often called *special revelation,* and the revelation of God in creation is often called *general revelation.* In homeschooling, we want to help our children approach every subject through the following paradigm:

Special Revelation
(A Scriptural Foundation)
↓
General Revelation
(The Subject Being Studied)
↓
Special Revelation
(Assessing the Subject According to Scripture)

Let's use a simple example. When our children begin to learn basic math, they learn the operation of addition and simple equations like 5+5=10. If we have been teaching our children well, they should come to mathematics already knowing there is a God in heaven, He created the world, and He is a God of order. As young children, they may not yet be able to verbalize these truths, but nevertheless they have been instilled into their hearts. Therefore, when they approach mathematics, they are not surprised to learn that our world is a world of design, a world of order, a world in which mathematic principles exist and hold true. They are approaching math from a worldview in which the idea of mathematical principles makes sense

The child then learns the operation of addition, and practices it over and over. The child grows in this skill. Over time, the child reaches mastery over simple addition. Our role as parents is to help our children see (in light of the Scriptural foundation) that addition was *God's* idea, He created it, and it is part of His glory in our world. We might ask our children to imagine a world in which 5+5 didn't equal 10, and how confusing and strange that would be. What if their five fingers on one hand and their five fingers on the other hand only equaled six fingers!

How different would their lives be? Our aim, in light of special revelation, is to help our children be grateful to God for addition.

The final stage is harder when our children are very young, but is a skill we should be seeking to develop in them as soon as they are capable of dialectic thought. This is the skill of assessing the new information according to Scripture. Even when our children are too young for analytical thought themselves, we can demonstrate this skill for them. Is addition *good?* Is it *helpful?* Do we see addition in the pages of the Bible? Can addition help us in fulfilling the commands God has given us?

Perhaps with addition we might point our children to the Christmas story, and how Jesus, who is fully God, added to Himself humanity. Just as adding one apple to one banana doesn't take away the banana, so Jesus never lost one bit of His divinity when He came as a baby in a manger. He was fully God, but He did add to Himself something new: a human body with a human nature. He became the God-man, fully God and fully man. Without addition, salvation would have been impossible! These are the kinds of connections we are after. These help our children see the world through a Scriptural worldview and have a better appreciation of each part of God's world. We will go much deeper into one method of cultivating this skill in the next chapter.

Worship
When we are homeschooling in faith, praying for God's blessing, and seeking to educate our children through the lens of Scripture, then *worship* should be a consistent, joyful mark of our homeschools. This is the aim: that our children would have regular moments in which their eyes are further opened to God's glory, their hearts are awed, and by grace, their faith is strengthened.

These moments need not last a long time. They may be only a few seconds, as our children have that experience of wonder, and then move on to the next assignment. It is right, however, that we encourage our children to stop and take a moment to thank God when those moments come. What a joy when our children are shooting up little darts of praise to God throughout their day!

If you are a musical family, or even if you are not, it might be fitting to occasionally take time to sing praises to God for what has been learned. At the end of the school day, mom might ask the children to

27

share some of what they studied that day. This might be a good opportunity for mom to help the children make some of the connections previously mentioned. Then, they could take time to sing a song of praise to God for His goodness. If doing this every day is too much, this could become a good practice for the end of each homeschool week.

Related to this, family dinner time can be a great way to include both parents in the God-centered discussions and praise. Going around the table, each child might share some of what they were working on that day, and the parents can help all the children think about those subjects in light of God. At the end of the discussion, dad might lead the family in a prayer of praise for His goodness.

Love

Finally, the God-centered homeschool should be marked by love. *"And above all these put on love, which binds everything together in perfect harmony"* (Colossians 3:14).

It is essential to the God-centered homeschool that the parents love God. We cannot give to our children what we do not first have ourselves. The fire must be blazing in our hearts first, and only then can we seek to set the hearts of our children aflame with Godward love. It should be our desire that in our daily words, attitudes, and actions our children would see that God is our highest love, our chief delight, the One who satisfies our souls.

It is also essential to the God-centered homeschool that there be a strong, warm love between the parents and their children. Seeking to point our children to God in every subject when we ourselves harbor anger or bitterness towards our children can have the opposite effect – it can turn them away from God and harden their hearts against Him. As parents, we must keep a close watch over the hearts of our children, and seek to ensure that they are secure in our love for them. Even when we must be firm and discipline them, it should be in the context of love. *"My son, give me your heart and let your eyes delight in my ways"* (Proverbs 23:26).

As parents, we should also seek to cultivate in ourselves and in our children a love for the *hunt*. I am referring here to the hunt in every subject for more of God and His glory. It is the hunt for connections, the hunger for that moment when the lightbulb turns on and the heart is suddenly awed by a fresh perception of God's goodness. We should work to form the godly habit in our children of seeking fresh encounters with God's glory that leave them wanting more and more. There is no shortage of supply – there are a billion ways in which He displays Himself in the physical world alone. He is a fountain of never-ending glory, the only object for the soul which will never disappoint.

Finding Help for God-Centered Homeschooling from Others

God is our strength as we seek to homeschool our children. Yet God works through means, and one of those means is other people. If we seek to be lone-ranger homeschoolers, we set ourselves up for discouragement and failure. There are at least three ways that we can find help for this journey from other people.

First, there is immeasurable value in being active members of a healthy, God-centered local church. It is in the church that we get to be part of a larger family of people who are seeking to grow together in knowing and enjoying God. It is there we hear the Word of God preached and applied to our souls by pastors who care for us. It is in a church that we gain brothers and sisters who love us enough to encourage us when we are down and admonish us when we are going astray. The local church is a greenhouse in which God especially blesses the means of grace - prayer, Scripture intake, Christian fellowship, etc. – so that their wonderful, life-giving effects are intensified in our lives. If you are not part of a healthy local church, that is step one in receiving God's help for your homeschool. If you are not sure what a truly healthy church looks like, I encourage you to read the little book *What is a Healthy Church?* by pastor Mark Dever.

Second, let me encourage you to pursue active participation in a local homeschooling community. There are tremendous benefits to uniting with other families who share the same goals for their homeschools. Homeschooling moms and dads can point each other to helpful resources, share lessons they have learned from their own experiences, pray with each other during difficult seasons, and rejoice together when God is especially blessing. For some families, participating in a like-minded homeschooling community may require driving an hour or more away from home, but the benefits typically outweigh the costs. My family has been participating in a Classical Conversations® community for more than ten years, and the encouragement we have found there has been vital to our homeschool journey. A homeschooling community can *never* be a replacement for the local church, and can never provide the same gifts to our souls that Christ provides in a local church context. The church is eternal; our homeschool communities are temporal. But it is a wonderful boon when we can be a part of both.

Third, we are blessed to live in a time when we have many written and audio/video resources that can serve the God-centered vision of our homeschooling. In later chapters, I will list a few resources that can aid us in discovering God's glory in various subjects of study. A few books for cultivating and maintaining a God-centered worldview include:

- *Knowing God* by J. I. Packer
- *Communion with God* by John Owen
- *The Pleasures of God: Meditations on God's Delight in Being God* by John Piper
- *When I Don't Desire God: How to Fight for Joy* by John Piper
- *Total Truth: Liberating Christianity from Its Cultural Captivity* by Nancy Pearcey
- *Saving Leonardo: A Call to Resist the Secular Assault on Mind, Morals, and Meaning* by Nancy Pearcey
- *Loving God with All Your Mind: Thinking as a Christian in the Postmodern World* by Gene Edward Veith, Jr.

3)

A God-Centered Method

"There is not a square inch in the whole domain of
our human existence over which Christ, who is sovereign
over all, does not cry, Mine!"
- Abraham Kuyper

In Romans 11, the Apostle Paul unpacks a mystery that has now been revealed. The mystery has to do with God's plan for saving His people from among Jews and Gentiles. God first revealed Himself and the way of salvation to the Jewish people. Through Jewish Christians (Paul, Peter, John, etc.), the gospel was spread to other nations, and today has reached the furthest corners of our world. Now, in a glorious turnabout, it is the *Gentiles* who are bringing the gospel back to Jews. Just as God worked through Israel to bring the gospel to the nations, God is now using the nations to bring a remnant of Jews to Jesus Christ. In this way, no one can boast in their ethnicity, but only in the sovereign wisdom of our gracious God.

In bringing his teaching on this subject to a close, Paul finds his heart bursting with wonder at God's ways with man. He cries out, "*Oh, the depth of the riches and wisdom and knowledge of God! How unsearchable are his judgments and how inscrutable his ways!*" (Romans 11:33). He then ends the discussion with a statement of praise that I believe is of great help to the home educator: "*For from him and through him and to him are all things. To him be glory forever. Amen*" (Romans 11:36). In this one verse we are given the ultimate purpose of everything, including all learning ("*to him be glory forever*"), as well as a framework through which we can approach any subject to accomplish that goal ("*from him and through him and to him*"). No other verse has proven more helpful to my own family's homeschooling journey than this one. I have found it to be a key that opens the door to God-centered homeschooling. I pray it will be of benefit to your family as well. Let's think about this verse.

First, we have here the ultimate goal of all learning. What is the goal? Heartfelt worship. *"To Him be glory forever!"* In every subject, our aim is that our children would be brought to a fresh sense of awe and wonder at the greatness of God. All things exist for His glory, and this means that there is no area of study in the universe which should not lead us or our children to stand amazed at our God.

Let us use trees as an example. There is so much that our children can learn about trees. They can learn some of the different types and varieties, and how to identify certain trees in their neighborhood. They can learn about the root system, or photosynthesis, or how to read tree rings to learn about weather events in past decades. Our children can learn about the roles that trees play in various ecosystems, and the animals that depend on trees for their homes. Yet if our children learn all of this, but do not see the creativity, wisdom, and power of God in a tree, then they have not yet learned the most important lesson. Knowledge that does not lead our children back to God is *vain* knowledge. It is incomplete in the most vital way. It is insufficient. Trees exist for the glory of God, as part of His handiwork, revealing something of Himself to us. If we have not yet seen God in our study of trees, we have not yet gotten the point!

This principle remains true whether our children are learning the letters of the alphabet or complicated chemical formulas. The "all things" of Romans 11:36 truly means *all* things. There is nothing we can consider in all creation that should not lead us to glorify God.

But how do we do this? How can we help our children to see God in the various subjects we study? Here is where the framework of Romans 11:36 proves so helpful. This verse shows us that we can always relate any subject to God in at least *three* ways: its origin (*from Him*), its role in God's providence (*through Him*), and its ultimate purpose (*to Him*). I call this "the God Grid", and the purpose of this chapter is to help us learn to apply it to any subject of study.

All Things are From God

Let's continue using trees as our example. How might we apply the God Grid? We can first point our children to God as the *origin* of trees. Trees were God's idea, part of His creative work. They are *from* God.

Imagine a mother taking her children on a nature hike. Along the way, nature guide in hand, she helps them learn to identify the various kinds of trees they see. How might she point her children to God as Creator? She might say, "What a wonderful God we have! Children, do you see how He chose to create so many different kinds of trees? Our God loves variety!" Or, as she explains to her children the roles that trees play in an environment, and how interdependent animals and plants (and humans!) are upon one another, she might say, "Do you see, kids, how wise our God is to create such a complex system?" As she tells the children about atoms, and how atoms form molecules, and how these can form living cells that produce bark and leaves and sap, the mother might remind the kids about the great power of God – not just over things we can see, but over the microscopic world as well. She might also point out that as wonderfully advanced as the human race is, only God can make a tree. These kinds of thoughts help children see the glory of God as the Designer and Creator of trees.

In applying this first part of the God Grid, the key is to first think about the nature of what is being studied, and then to draw conclusions about what that nature tells us about God. As I have said previously, making these connections is a *dialectic* skill, so when our children are very young it will be us parents who will lead the way in demonstrating by example. As our children get older, they can grow into this skill and make it their own. Applying the God Grid through conversation also helps our children grow in the skill of rhetoric, as they learn to better articulate the discoveries they are making.

Two questions may prove helpful here. First, we lead our children to ask, "What are some facts about _____?" Second, we ask, "What do these facts teach us about the God who made _____?" Continuing with our present example, we might ask our children to discover facts about trees. They can do this through their own observation, through reading books, and in many other ways. They might even make a list of facts about trees:

1. There are many different kinds of trees.

2. Trees need water and sunshine to grow.

3. Trees produce oxygen which helps us breathe.

After they have made their list, we can then guide them in looking at each fact and asking what it teaches us about God.

1. There are many different kinds of trees. God is very creative.

2. Trees need water and sunshine to grow. It is God who causes trees and all living things to grow.

3. Trees produce oxygen which help us breathe. It is God who lets us live.

These conclusions about God are very simple (they were supplied by my eight-year-old son), but they are wonderful insights for a young child. As our children develop and mature, the insights and conversations become more in-depth and wonderful. We might not have our older children make lists like this, but we join with them conversationally in asking what the nature of the subject they are studying teaches us about God.

All Things are Through God
Thankfully, I have seen in my interactions with other Christian homeschool families that many of them are already practicing the skill of pointing their children to God as *Creator* to at least some degree. It is not unusual for many homeschool moms or dads to remind their children that what they are learning about came ultimately from God. Sadly, many families stop there. Yet Romans 11:36 reminds us that all things are not only *from* God, but also *through* God. God sustains all things and includes them as a part of the great story that He is working in the world. It has become cliché, but history really is *His story*, and every part of the created world has a role to play in that story. Once we understand this, we find another door opening to us through which we can see much, much more of God's glory in even the simplest of subjects.

As with the first part of the God Grid, I would suggest that there are two questions that may be particularly helpful in this regard. First, we can ask, "What role does this person / place / thing / idea play in

Scripture?" Second, we can ask, "What role does this person / place / thing / idea play in history?"

Let's continue thinking about trees as our example. What role do trees play in Scripture? Trees play a *massive* role in Scripture. Our imaginary mother has the opportunity to remind her children about the many trees in the Garden of Eden that were given graciously by God to Adam and Eve for their enjoyment and the sustenance of their lives. She might remind them of one particular tree in that Garden, the Tree of the Knowledge of Good and Evil, and how one bite from that tree plunged the human race into darkness and sin. She might remind them how Jesus Christ came and died on a tree, giving His life that sinners would be saved. She could even point them to the book of Revelation, which speaks of the Tree of Life, and how those who are in Christ get to eat of that tree and live forever with Him in heaven. God's great story of redemption is a story in which trees play a major part. Every tree we see can be a reminder to us of the gospel. Every tree is an opportunity to point our children to Jesus.

There are many other roles that trees play in Scripture. Perhaps as the children are learning about the root system and how trees are nourished, the mother might point them to Psalm 1. There we read of the blessed man who is *"like a tree planted by streams of water that yields its fruit in season, and its leaf does not wither"* (Psalm 1:3). How can we be like a fruitful tree? How can we flourish and thrive? *"His delight is in the law of the LORD, and on his law he meditates day and night"* (Psalm 1:2). In other words, the roots of a tree remind us that we too must root ourselves in the truths of God's word. When we are firmly rooted, we too can bear much fruit for God.

One more example. In Matthew 12:33-34 Jesus said, *"Either make the tree good and its fruit good, or make the tree bad and its fruit bad, for the tree is known by its fruit...For out of the abundance of the heart the mouth speaks."* Just as a healthy tree produces healthy fruit, and an unhealthy tree produces bad fruit, so also our outward words and actions flow from what is in our hearts. If we want to be people who speak kindness to others, then we must work to foster kindness in our hearts. This is a valuable lesson to learn from trees. Homeschool moms and dads should pray that the Holy Spirit would bring to their minds Scriptures like these as they talk with their children about whatever they are studying.

We could say much, much more about how God uses trees in Scripture to teach important spiritual lessons. However, we also have our second question: What role have trees played in history? This is an opportunity to think about God's providence, and the things He has done in the past.

What stories might our imaginary mom tell her kids? Perhaps she will tell them the story of Thor's Oak, and how God used the destruction of that idolized tree to bring many Hessians to Christ. Perhaps she will tell them the old myth about George Washington and the cherry tree, and his purported statement "I cannot tell a lie." She might tell them about Isaac Newton's apple tree in Woolsthorpe, England, or the Liberty Tree in Boston, or Anne Frank's chestnut tree in Amsterdam. It is incredible to think about all the ways God has used trees in the course of history.

We should be careful not to forget our personal histories. Our imaginary mother might tell her children about certain trees she remembers from her own childhood. I personally remember several trees from my own childhood that bring back precious memories: picking up pecans under the large trees near my grandparents' house, sitting with my grandmother on the outdoor swing underneath the large black walnut tree in her backyard, watching a hurricane bring down trees onto people's houses during hurricane Opal. Sharing these stories with our children can be just as vital to their formation as learning the parts of a tree, for they help shape their character, strengthen family unity, and enlarge their vision of God. Moreover, these discussions help connect whatever the children are studying to the rest of life, integrating all subjects together into a unified whole that exists for the glory of God.

As our children mature, these conversations about Scripture and history should become less one-sided. Instead of mom or dad dominating the conversation, the children themselves help make connections between the subjects of study and the roles they play in God's providence.

All Things are For God
Finally, Romans 11:36 reminds us that all things exist *"for God."* This means that the ultimate purpose of everything in the universe is to serve His plan of displaying His worth and goodness. In applying this part of

the God Grid, there are two further questions that are helpful: First, does this person / place / thing / idea have a merely temporal purpose, or also an eternal one? This question is especially helpful in helping our kids learn to be heavenly-minded, and to view all things in light of an eternal perspective. Second, we can lead them to ask, "How might we use this person / place / thing / idea to bring further glory to God?"

Let's apply these questions to trees. First, do trees have only a temporal purpose, or will they continue to exist and have purpose in the world to come? Our answers to this kind of question will vary from family to family because of differing theological perspectives, and there will often be a degree of speculation in our answers. In teaching my own children, I would point out that the Bible speaks of the eternal Heaven as "the new earth", seeming to imply that many of the features of this earth will be in Heaven, only without any of the effects of sin. This gives me reason to believe that there will be trees in heaven, and perhaps more glorious trees than any yet seen on earth. Compared to the California redwoods, that is a spectacular prospect to consider!

Our imaginary mother might help her children answer the question in a different way. She might tell them that she is unsure about whether or not trees will be in heaven, but she knows this: we will be *singing* about a tree for all eternity. In Revelation 5:9-10 we learn that the saints in heaven joyfully praise the Lord Jesus Christ in song, and that the central theme of their praises is His redeeming death on the cross:

> *Worthy are you to take the scroll*
> *and to open its seals,*
> *for you were slain, and by your blood you ransomed*
> *people for God from every tribe and language and*
> *people and nation,*
> *and you have made them a kingdom and priests to our*
> *God, and they shall reign on the earth.*

Second, we would lead our children to consider how trees can be used to bring further glory to God. The answers here are numerous. Our mother might talk with her children about the many products in which the wood or cellulose of trees is essential: lipstick, toilet paper, football helmets, candles, tires, cough syrup, etc. When we use any of these items with gratitude, we bring glory to God. Our mother might talk to her kids about paper, and how God has especially used books both to bring many people to Christ and to grow them up in the faith. The Bible itself often comes to us in the form of a book with paper which comes from trees. She might also draw their attention to God's command in Genesis that mankind care for the earth, and mention how we can glorify God as caretakers of trees, making wise decisions as stewards of this precious resource.

One of the wonderful benefits of these questions is that often your children will have answers that you had not yet considered, and the conversation will go in surprising directions. It is not just our children, but often we as parents who find ourselves in unexpected adoration of our God.

Honing and Imparting These Skills
Let me remind you again that though we have used trees as an example, this framework can be used with any subject. The *all things* of Romans 11:36 holds true in every circumstance. Some subjects are more difficult than others, and require us to think a little harder to make the connections, but this often adds to the joy of the hunt. Every subject points us to God in terms of *origin, providence,* and *purpose.*

As you think about using the God Grid your own homeschool, there are four further points I'd like you to consider: First, remember that this is not the *only* way to strive for God-centeredness in your homeschool, but merely *one* way that I believe can be helpful. Second, the best way to strengthen this skill of seeing God in every subject is to *practice.* The more we attempt to apply the God Grid to various parts of our world, the better we will get at seeing and savoring the grandeur of our God everywhere. This skill is like a muscle – the more it is employed, the stronger it gets.

Third, as our children grow and learn, we should allow them to take on the task of making the connections themselves. Discoveries are always more meaningful when we have made them ourselves. Also, the more practice our children get at using this skill, the more their own souls will benefit. As they grow and mature both physically and spiritually, you will find that their ability to make these connections strengthens and their insights deepen. Some of these wonderful conversations alone make every sacrifice we have made to homeschool worthwhile!

Fourth, once our children have become capable of analytical thinking, applying the God Grid can be either a *solitary* or a *corporate* activity. That is, we can give our students the God Grid questions and allow them to answer them on their own, or we can engage them in conversation. When our children are looking for God in a subject as a solitary exercise, we might assign them to write a paper or prepare an oral presentation through which they can share their discoveries. There is a place for both solitary and corporate learning in this regard, though I would suggest that the higher joys lie in God-centered conversation and making discoveries alongside others rather than on our own.

Who Has Time for This?!
As you have been reading this chapter, you might have been thinking, "Who has time for this?" Most of us live hectic lives, and simply getting our children to complete their assignments can be trying enough. Once we add looking for God's glory into the mix of every subject of study, haven't we added a whole new layer of work for our children (and often for ourselves?).

Let me respond with three answers. First, we must always keep before our eyes the purpose of our children's education. The ultimate aim is that our children would know and enjoy God. If we content ourselves with anything less than this, we are failing to truly give our children a *God*-centered education.

Second, let me remind you of the warning I gave at the end of the first chapter. The "get-it-done" mentality is a great enemy to God-centered homeschooling. We must work to rid ourselves of this mentality, and learn instead to embrace a model of education in which our children *savor* the subjects they are learning. Too many homeschool families are pushing their children along, wanting their children to be the next Doogie Howser. In doing so, they are robbing the children of the opportunity to truly see God in their studies, and to have their souls enriched. This is why I suggest that it is ultimately better for our children to study less more deeply, and to see God in those subjects, than to study more, superficially, and to miss His glory altogether. If our homeschooling doesn't allow our children time to be still and know God, then perhaps we need to let some areas of study go.

Third, as I mentioned in the second chapter, there are ways to add these God-centered discussions to your homeschool that do not disrupt your established patterns and rhythms. Applying the God Grid to the day's studies with your children can be done at the end of a homeschool day or week, or at family dinner (when both parents can often be part of the conversation.)

A Big Vision of God for Future Trials
One of the benefits of teaching our children to see God in every subject is that their own view of God grows. Christians with small views of God have little confidence in Him when trials come. They are given to fear and anxiety. As much as we would like to spare our children from heartache and suffering, the reality is that they will face their share of obstacles and disappointments. By giving our children a God-centered education, we help them see that the God of the Bible is also the God of "real life", the God actively and intricately involved in every aspect of their lives. Having seen His creativity, wisdom, power, goodness, justice, compassion, and love in a thousand ways throughout their education, they will be better prepared to trust Him when it is hardest to do so. A. W. Tozer famously said, "What comes into our minds when we think about God is the most important thing about us." A God-centered education helps our children have *mighty* thoughts of God, and not *wimpy* thoughts that offer little comfort.

As a father, it is easy for me to become a little uneasy when I think about my sons. It is clear to me that the Christian-friendly culture that I have known for much of my life is not the culture they are going to know for most of theirs. Hostility to our faith seems to be increasing. Biblical ideas that were once widely accepted are now deemed old-fashioned or even hateful. The temptations on my sons to forsake Christ are going to be very strong.

What can I do to prepare my boys for the days God has prepared for them? One of the most important is helping them see that the God we worship is *worthy* of their allegiance. If by God's grace I can instill in their souls a vision of God that is greater than the allurements of this world or even the value of their own lives, I will have prepared them well. Elizabeth Elliot once wrote, "The world cries for men who are strong; strong in conviction, strong to lead, to stand, to suffer." My desire is that my sons would become such men. If they can see God's worth not only in the pages of the Bible but in every direction they set their eyes, then God may grant them to be ready to stand no matter what trials come their way.

A Missional Education

There is another benefit to helping our children see God in the "all things" of this world. We do not know what callings God will bring into the lives of our children. If we try and cater the content of our children's education to what we think God may call them to do, we may discover in the future that we were way off the mark. I think of the parent who teaches her child Spanish, thinking it might help that child to one day minister to Mexican immigrants in the U.S., only for the child to be called by God into missionary work in China. We simply do not know what God has in store for our children.

However, whatever God calls our children to be or do, the lessons of a God-centered education are *always* applicable. They equip our children to be thoughtful, well-reasoned, winsome servants for Christ in any vocation. Applying the God Grid gives our children practice at clear and godly thinking, something they will need the rest of their lives. It is also an avenue to give our children practice at rhetorical skills such as meaningful conversation, respectful debate, oral presentations, and persuasive essays or reports. There are few callings for which such skills are not very valuable. If the ultimate purpose of every calling is that we glorify God, then this method helps our children prepare to succeed in fulfilling that purpose. This is the goal of the God Grid – that our children's hearts, minds, and character be shaped by learning to behold God everywhere and in everything. What Paul wrote about beholding God's glory in Scripture applies no less to beholding His glory in all creation: *"And we all, with unveiled face, beholding the glory of the Lord, are being transformed into the same image from one degree of glory to another"* (2nd Corinthians 3:18a).

The God Grid
(Sample from homeschool students[4])

*"For from him and through him and to him are all things.
To him be glory forever. Amen."*
- Romans 11:36

ELECTRICITY

From God (Origin)
1. What are some facts about electricity?

- Electricity is one of the four forces of creation.
- Like Aslan in the Chronicles of Narnia, electricity is good but not safe.
- Electricity is produced by the movement of electrons between atoms.
- Light is produced through electricity.
- We have become reliant on electricity for modern conveniences.

2. What do these facts teach us about God who made electricity?

- God is wise to have created such a complex world.
- God is loving to give us electricity to help ease our discomforts.
- God is supreme – He is able to produce electricity all over the universe whenever He pleases.
- God is omnipresent – He produces electricity wherever He pleases.
- Like electricity, God is good but not safe.

Through God (Providence)

3. What role does electricity play in Scripture?

- Lightning expresses the power of God, especially at the giving of the Ten Commandments at Mount Sinai.
- Light, which is produced through electricity, is used as a metaphor for righteousness.
- Jesus taught that His return would be like a flash of lightning (Matthew 24:27; Luke 17:24).
- The end of the world is depicted in Revelation with lightning (Revelation 11:19; 16:18).

4. What role does lightning play in history?

- Harnessing electricity advances cultures.
- People such as Benjamin Franklin have been discovering the mysteries of electricity throughout history.
- Electricity has been used to bring about great scientific discoveries, especially through electrolysis.

For God (Purpose)

5. Does electricity have an eternal purpose?

- Unsure. Since the eternal heaven is described as a "New Earth", it is possible that there will be electricity in heaven.

6. How might we use electricity to further glorify God?

- Electricity can be used in many practical ways to honor God, including using it to meet people's physical needs, to power worship bands, or to present the gospel online.
- We glorify God by being thankful for electricity.

The God Grid
(Use this blank grid to give it a try yourself!)

*"For from him and through him and to him are all things.
To him be glory forever. Amen."*
- Romans 11:36

RIVERS

From God (Origin)
1. What are some facts about rivers?

_____
_____
_____
_____
_____

2. What do these facts teach us about God who made rivers?

_____
_____
_____
_____
_____

Through God (Providence)
3. What role do rivers play in Scripture?

_____
_____
_____
_____
_____

4. What role do rivers play in history?

_____
_____
_____
_____
_____

For God (Purpose)
5. Do rivers have an eternal purpose?

_____
_____
_____
_____
_____

6. How might we use rivers to further glorify God?

_____
_____
_____
_____
_____

The God Grid
(Use this blank grid to give it a try yourself!)

*"For from him and through him and to him are all things.
To him be glory forever. Amen."*
- Romans 11:36

EARTHQUAKES

From God (Origin)
1. What are some facts about earthquakes?

_____
_____
_____
_____
_____

2. What do these facts teach us about God who made earthquakes?

_____
_____
_____
_____
_____

Through God (Providence)
3. What role do earthquakes play in Scripture?

_____
_____
_____
_____
_____

4. What role do earthquakes play in history?

_____
_____
_____
_____
_____

For God (Purpose)
5. Does earthquakes have an eternal purpose?

_____
_____
_____
_____
_____

6. How might we use earthquakes to further glorify God?

_____
_____
_____
_____
_____

4)

God-Centered Math

*"So teach us to number our days that we
may get a heart of wisdom."*
- Psalm 90:12

The ancient Greeks were on a quest to discover the fundamental element that makes up and unifies all things. It was their contention that everything – rivers and mountains and babies and olive trees – were formed of this primary element. But what could it be?

One of the earliest Greek philosophers, Thales of Miletus, suggested that it was water. A successor of his, Anaximenes, argued that it was air, or some air-like ethereal substance. Heraclitus, in the 5th century BC, rejoined that it was fire. It was a mathematician named Pythagoras, however, who came closest to the truth.

Pythagoras was a lover of music. He discovered that strings of varied lengths, when plucked together, produced different harmonies – some concordant and others discordant. He learned that a string of the same width and tension, but half the size of another, would produce the same tone an octave higher. Ratios, he realized, created harmony.

Everywhere Pythagoras looked in the natural world he saw harmonies (on the earth below and in the heavens above), and he therefore deduced that mathematical principles lie behind everything. According to Pythagoras, *number* was the elusive element that gives order to everything.

After this discovery, it became obvious to Pythagoras and his adherents that there must be a connection between the principles of mathematics and the divine. Some of his followers actually began to worship the first four numbers as gods. Pythagoras himself was worshiped as a saint, and the math-oriented religion that he began (called Pythagoreanism) influenced many, including Plato.

Pythagoras was onto something. There is a connection between God and the mathematical principles that bring order to our world.

Pythagoras did not have the light of Scripture, and as Christians we know that math is not to be worshiped. But there is a real sense in which math is divine. It is the language God spoke at creation that gave form to the universe.

> *Let all the earth fear the LORD;*
> *let all the inhabitants of the world stand in awe of him!*
> *For he spoke, and it came to be;*
> *he commanded, and it stood firm.*

Mathematical principles have their origin in God, spring forth from Him, and give our universe its shape and contours, holding the physical world together. When we see math rightly, we cannot help but look to God in wonder and worship.

A Personal Testimony

I did not always see math this way. As a child, I found math to be loathsome. My early detestation for math was not because I struggled with the principles, though that certainly was true in the higher math of trigonometry and calculus, but because I simply found no joy in solving the assigned problems. Like many children, I often wondered what these math problems had to do with real life. How was knowing the formula for the area of a trapezoid going to serve me and my future? I viewed math as a waste of my time.

I confess that this distaste for math continued even into adulthood. My math professors in college did not help matters, not even attempting to make their classes interesting. Once I graduated, I largely kept math at arm's length, only using the basic math required for daily life.

In His providence, God brought into our church a graduate level professor of mathematics. This Christian lady had a strong love for God *and* a strong love for math. I will never forget how she explained to us the beauty of God that she saw in the complex equations and formulas with which she worked. I had always seen more of the *devil* in complex equations, not God! Yet now my eyes were opened to the fact that math is more than a necessity of our world – it is an expression of God Himself.

Both as a homeschool father and as a tutor for other students, I have since tried to find ways to help students see more of God in the math principles they are learning. I am thankful for those people and books God has brought into my life to help in this endeavor. For the rest of this chapter, we will practice using the God Grid to see God's glory in math.

Math Is from God
First, we need to choose a mathematical truth for us to think about. We could choose a *law* of mathematics, such as the distributive law:

$$a (b + c) = (a \cdot b) + (a \cdot c)$$

We could choose a mathematical formula, such as the Pythagorean theorem:

$$a^2 + b^2 = c^2$$

We could also choose a foundational math concept, such as the fact that any plural number intrinsically combines both *unity* and *diversity*. Throughout your child's education, there will be opportunities to apply the God Grid to many aspects of math.

For the sake of introducing this skill, we will focus our attention on a very simple equation that we talked about in chapter two: 5+5=10.

Now, what are some facts that we can list about this equation?[5] The first fact that your children might observe is that this equation is *true*. That is wonderfully correct. Beginning there, we can lead them to consider many more facts about this equation. As you will see, even the practice of observing these facts will teach them about far more than just math:

5+5=10 *is* true. It was true yesterday. It is true today. It will be true tomorrow. There has never been a time and never will be when this equation does not hold true. Therefore, we can state that 5+5=10 is *eternal*.

5+5=10 is true in this room in which I am typing, and it is true wherever you are as you read this. It is true in New Jersey. It is true in Indonesia. It is true on the International Space Station. We could select any solar system anywhere in the vast universe, and it would still remain accurate that five planets added to five more planets equals ten planets. Therefore, 5+5-10 is *omnipresent*.

5+5=10 is true above and beyond its particular applications. If there were no planets, no people, no elephants, no pencils, or anything else in the physical universe to apply our equation to, it would still nevertheless be true. It is true even outside of time and space. In that sense, 5+5=10 is *transcendent*.

Granting that 5+5=10 is true in an abstract, transcendent sense, it is also practically true in a thousand expressions within our daily lives. Five fingers plus five fingers is ten fingers. Five miles plus five miles equals ten miles. This equation is not merely an abstract truth, but it also helps shape our lives right here and right now, in space and in time. 5+5=10 is *imminent*.

Can 5+5=10 ever change and not be true? No. It is as fixed as God Himself. It is unchangeable, or what we might call *immutable*.

5+5=10 is a truth that we see expressions of all around us. Yet the truth itself is not a physical *thing*. It exists in the realm of principle, in the realm of ideas. We can hold *examples* of this truth in our hand (say, ten marbles), but the equation itself is not something we can touch or handle. It is an ideational truth. It is *immaterial*.

Similarly, though we see expressions of our equation all around us, the truth itself has no visible form. We can express it in writing using Hindu-Arabic numerals or Roman numerals, but the truth itself is fundamentally *invisible*.

Surely by this point it is clear that this list of facts about our equation tells us about more than just the equation. We are discovering that the attributes of math mirror the attributes of God. In leading our children to think through this (in a way corresponding to their maturity and ability to think critically), we should ask them *why* they think God and a simple equation like 5+5=10 have so much in common? But before we move on to that question ("What do these facts tell us about the God who made 5+5=10?"), let's make our list of facts a bit longer.

5+5=10 is an equation that we can depend upon. Because it is always true, it will never let us down. It is *faithful*.

5+5=10 is a truth that was not invented by any mathematician or scientist. It was discovered (or simply known) by the very first humans – Adam and Eve. I would guess that when Adam met Eve, they instinctively knew that the one plus the other equaled two. Basic equations were obvious to them. It did not matter what Adam and Eve applied them to, the principles of math held true. Today, you and I can name ten million different unified objects, and it will always be true that five of them plus five of them equals ten. There is nothing that can shake this truth. Everything submits to it. In that sense, 5+5=10 has *sovereignty*. It reigns over the universe.

5+5=10 is a truth that we as human beings can know and understand. It is *knowable*.

5+5=10 also has depths and mysteries to it that boggle our minds. Why is this true everywhere and in every place? Why do the laws of mathematics always hold true, and why do we have these laws and not others? Why doesn't five plus five equal *eleven* everywhere and at all times? Indeed, the more we dig into even the most basic math, the more we begin to see that there is an *incomprehensibility* to the simplest equations. We can never fully plumb the depths of even the most basic mathematical truth.

We could not live in a world where 5+5=10 was untrue or changing. It is the consistency of mathematical truths that makes all creation, the plans of God, and our lives possible. Moreover, this truth never lies to us and never deceives us. Therefore, we can say that 5+5=10 is *good*. It is pure – there is no deceit in it.

5+5=10 is also a truth that brings harmony and symmetry into this world and into our lives. It brings order and coherence and agreement into the world. Therefore, we can say that 5+5=10 is *beautiful*.

Finally, what happens when people try to live as if five plus five does *not* equal ten? For example, what happens when people try to live with an unbalanced budged for their homes or businesses? What happens when people try to make five plus five equal *eleven* so that they can purchase what they want? There are consequences. There is debt. Our lives reap negative consequences when we try to break the laws of math. In that sense, 5+5=10 is *righteous*.

Let's look at our list of facts about 5+5=10. Our equation is…

True	Eternal	Omnipresent
Transcendent	Imminent	Immutable
Immaterial	Invisible	Faithful
Sovereign	Knowable	Incomprehensible
Good	Beautiful	Righteous

Now, these facts could be stated about *all* mathematical truths or principles, so your student would not need to list all of these each time they apply the God Grid. Instead, they might choose one or two of these, or focus on other facts not listed here.

The second question of our God Grid asks what we can learn about God from the facts that we have listed. The underlying principle here is that math is the language of God given to the physical world, and therefore these characteristics of math reflect *His* characteristics. With that in mind, our children can focus on any of these facts and make the connection to God's character. For example, just as 5+5=10 is always faithful and will never let us down, remaining true for us in all circumstances, so our God is also faithful. He will always fulfill His Word just as He has promised, and He will never betray our trust. He is *worthy* of our trust, *worthy* of our confidence in Him, for He is as faithful as the equations He created.

Math Is through God

Following our grid, the next two questions provide *vast* opportunities for engaging discussions. You will enjoy hearing your children's imaginations as they answer these questions.

First, what role does 5+5=10 play in Scripture? Our children might point to numerous examples:

- Five chapters plus five chapters equals ten chapters.
- Had there been five plus five righteous men in Sodom, God would not have destroyed it (Genesis 18:32).
- After the first five plagues, God brought five more upon Egypt, totaling ten plagues (Exodus 7-12).
- The Ten Commandments are the sum of five commandments plus five commandments.
- In the Parable of the Talents, one servant is given five talents by his master. Through wise trading, he makes five talents more. When the master returns, the servant presents to him the sum: ten talents (cf. Matthew 25:14-30).
- There were five plus five lepers who came to Jesus to be healed, though only one returned to say thanks (Luke 17:11-19).

Homeschool parents might choose to enlarge the question, asking "What role does *addition* play in Scripture?" instead of the specific equation 5+5=10. Focusing on operations, principles, or other elements of math rather than specific numerical problems help our children make more connections at this step in the grid. The possible answers here are too many to count, but a few might include:

- Adam plus Eve equaled two people. Marriage is an example of addition.
- Adam and Eve had children, adding to their family. Childbearing is an example of addition.
- God promised Abraham many descendants, which could only occur through addition.
- As each pair (or group of seven) animals entered the ark, the ark became fuller through addition.
- The Great Commission calls Christians to spread the gospel, that Christ's kingdom might grow through addition.

Sometimes these connections bring new insights for our children. For example, one child might wonder why God said He would *multiply* Abraham's descendants if these descendants could only come into Abraham's family through *addition?* The answer, of course, is that multiplication is merely repeated addition. These kinds of discoveries help our children to own the truths they are learning, and to avoid the snare I fell into as a child – thinking that math had little to do with real life.

The next question of the God Grid asks, "What role does 5+5=10 play in history?" Like the question before, the potential answers are only limited by our children's imaginations. Because math is so universally interwoven into every facet of our world, there are countless possibilities of correct responses. One child might mention that after five states entered the Union, five more entered, with Virginia becoming the tenth state. Another might point out that the Bill of Rights is made up of five amendments plus five amendments, composing the first ten amendments to the U.S. Constitution. Or, you can enlarge the question to ask about the role of addition in history, only increasing the variety of potential answers your children might provide.

Remember, the goal in these questions is to help our children see how this mathematical truth created by God has continued to bring order and sense to our world throughout history. During these discussions, we might point out to them the foolishness of those who argue that our world is the result of chance. How ironic that esteemed professional scientists use the orderly principles of mathematics to try and prove that there is no ultimate design or meaning in the universe! Their very tools argue against their theories of chance. Or we might point out to our children how all equations, including 5+5=10, stand against those who want to argue that all truth is relative and that we can each have our own truth. These equations remind us that postmodern thinking is false and fails as a workable perspective for life. Ultimately, we want our children to see that every application of math in the course of human history bears the fingerprints of God. This truly is our Father's world.

Math Is for God

Having thought about our equation in terms of its origin and what it teaches us about God, as well as in terms of God's providence both in Scripture and general history, we can now think about it in terms of God's *purpose*.

Does 5+5=10 have an *eternal* purpose, or merely a temporal one? Can we expect this equation to still be true in Heaven and the age to come?

These questions can be fun to think about. I would suggest that our equation will be as true in heaven as it is on earth, because its truthfulness does not ultimately lie in any created thing, but in God who is the same forever. In Revelation 21, when John describes his vision of Paradise, he speaks using *numbers*. We are told that the heavenly city has twelve gates with twelve angels and twelve inscriptions (v. 12). We are told that the wall of the city has twelve foundations inscribed with the twelve names of the twelve apostles (v. 14). The city is described as a cube, being of equal length, width, and height, with each wall measuring 144 cubits (vv. 16-17). Whether we take this description of Heaven to be literal or figurative, it seems to indicate that mathematical principles hold true in the world to come.

A further confirmation of this is the Bible's teaching (contrary to some eastern religions) that we will remain individuals for all eternity.

We will not lose our distinctive identities in heaven, nor will we be absorbed with others into some amorphous whole. Instead, heaven will be filled with millions of individual people retaining their individuality. When five of these individuals are added to five more, we have every reason to believe the sum will remain ten. Heaven, like earth, will be a world of math.

How might we use 5+5=10 to further glorify God? Your children will again have many possible answers to choose from. Perhaps we save five dollars, and then another five dollars, in order to give ten dollars to the local children's home. We might learn to count to ten before we speak to keep ourselves from responding harshly to someone. If we tell five people about Jesus, and then each of them tell someone, we will have reached ten people with the Good News.

Helps for God-Centered Math

Before closing this chapter, let me remind you that though we have used a simple equation as our example, the God Grid can be very useful in discovering God-centered insights and having God-centered conversations about much higher mathematical concepts. I actually recommend using math operations, terms, laws, and theorems rather than specific math problems or equations as we have done here.[6] Consider applying the Grid to fractions, for example, or to averages, or to the number *googol*. In every case, let your goal be for you and your children to love the Lord your God with all your minds, seeing His glory in every truth.

As an advocate for classical education, let me urge you to ensure that your children are not just learning how to solve math problems, but how to speak the language of math. It is in writing or speaking about math that we can better lead others to see God's glory in numbers and formulas, and our children will be better equipped to do this if they have had practice. The skill of rhetoric begins by learning the grammar of a subject, and this means learning the vocabulary of math. I suggest that we do best to use math curriculums that have glossaries, and give our children opportunities to articulate in writing and speech the principles that they are learning.

Finally, I urge homeschool parents to supplement their math curriculums with books that connect math principles to history and real people. Some of the best discussions I have had with homeschool students in this regard were about men such as Euclid, Pythagoras, John Philoponus, and Isaac Newton. Together we learned about these men, their mathematical discoveries, and then practiced applying the principles they discovered ourselves. Connecting math to real people, times, and places can help our children see the wisdom of God in the way all the many subjects of study integrate together into one God-centered whole.

Here are a few recommended resources:

- *Redeeming Mathematics: A God-Centered Approach* by Vern Poythress
- *Mathematics: Is God Silent?* by James Nickel
- *Arithmetic for Parents* by Ron Aharoni
- *Mathematicians are People, Too: Stories from the Lives of Great Mathematicians* by Luetta and Wilma Reimer
- *Mathematics in Everyday Things* by William Vergara
- *Agnesi to Zeno: Over 100 Vignettes from the History of Math* by Sanderson M. Smith

The God Grid

(Sample from homeschool students[4])

*"For from him and through him and to him are all things.
To him be glory forever. Amen."*
- Romans 11:36

GEOMETRY

From God (Origin)
1. What are some facts about geometry?

- Geometry is the study of the math principles concerning space (lines, points, etc.)
- Though many people may not know the rules of geometry, they use them and live in them every day.
- Geometric rules remain true wherever you go.
- Geometric rules were created by God.

2. What do these facts teach us about God who made geometry?

- God is truthful, since the rules that come from Him are always true.
- God is a God of order and not chaos.
- God has massive knowledge.
- God is wise in His ordering of the universe.

Through God (Providence)
3. What role does geometry play in Scripture?

- Geometry was used in measurements, such as Noah's ark and the construction of the tabernacle and Temple.
- God sometimes speaks in geometric terms (i.e., Numbers 34:7-8, 10; Psalm 16:6)
- From the very beginning, in the Garden of Eden, there was a sense of east and west.

- Paul's travels on the Mediterranean Sea would have required geometry.

4. What role does geometry play in history?

- Geometry was the first studied branch of mathematics.
- Archimedes used geometry to develop culture and defeat an army.
- The door at Plato's Academy was engraved with the statement: "Let no one ignorant of geometry enter here."
- Geometry led to simplifying life and explaining pre-known concepts.

For God (Purpose)
5. Does geometry have an eternal purpose?

- In Revelation, the New Jerusalem is described as a perfect cube.
- Since we will continue to have physical bodies in the age to come, and since the eternal heaven seems to be a physical place ("A New Earth"), it is likely that geometric principles will remain as true then as they are now.

6. How might we use geometry to further glorify God?

- We can thank God for the order He has given our world.
- We can study geometry to learn more about God Himself.
- We can wonder at the infinity of space.
- Geometry can be used in many ways to benefit evangelical projects (ex: World Changers Ministry builds houses as part of their gospel work.)

The God Grid
(Sample from homeschool students[4])

"For from him and through him and to him are all things.
To him be glory forever. Amen."
- Romans 11:36

PI

From God (Origin)
1. What are some facts about Pi?

- The number Pi is the ratio of the circumference of a circle to its diameter. Whatever the size of the circle, the circumference divided by the diameter will always equal Pi.
- Pi= 3.14159...
- Pi is an infinite number, impossible to be fully calculated.
- Pi is an irrational number, impossible to be written as a simple fraction.
- The Greek letter π is used for this number, also giving its name.

2. What do these facts teach us about God who made Pi?

- Since God knows all things, He knows all the digits of Pi.
- Since Pi is infinite, and God knows it completely, His knowledge must be infinite in scope.
- Like Pi, God is constant and never changing.
- Like Pi, there is both a simplicity and a complexity to God.
- God is an intelligent designer, weaving Pi into so many aspects of our lives.

Through God (Providence)

3. What role does Pi play in Scripture?

- We see the number Pi (estimated down to 3.0) in 1st Kings 7:23, describing the Temple furnishings.
- Since the sun and the earth and the vast multitude of stars and planets in the universe are orbs, Pi was greatly used by God at the Creation of the world.

4. What role does Pi play in history?

- It has existed since the beginning of Creation.
- Many people throughout history have tried to determine Pi, from the ancient Babylonians and Egyptians to current mathematicians.
- Since Pi is a geometric formulation related to circles, as well as a number between 3 and 4 on the number line, Pi is everywhere in human history – wherever there have been circles or lines!
- In 2010, mathematician Fabrice Bellard announced that he had determined Pi to 2.7 trillion digits.

For God (Purpose)

5. Does Pi have an eternal purpose?

- Since numbers are in everything, we expect Pi to continue to exist into eternity.

6. How might we use Pi to further glorify God?

- We can use Pi and the attributes of math to point skeptics to God as an Intelligent Designer.
- We honor God as His image-bearers by working with math and acknowledging that every principle and number (including Pi) come from Him.

The God Grid
(Sample from homeschool students[4])

"For from him and through him and to him are all things.
To him be glory forever. Amen."
- Romans 11:36

THE FIBONACCI CODE

From God (Origin)
1. What are some facts about the Fibonacci Code?

- The Fibonacci Code appears throughout the created world, usually in the form of spirals found in the branching of trees, the flowering of various fruits and vegetables, the placement of leaves on stems, rams' horns, etc.
- The Fibonacci Code is sometimes called "Nature's Numbering System."
- The beginning of the Code is 1, 1, 2, 3, 5, 8, 13, 21, 34...
- Each number of the Code is found by adding the two previous numbers.

2. What do these facts teach us about God who made the Fibonacci Code?

- God loves order – He has woven this consistent pattern into nature itself.
- God loves variety – He uses this pattern in many different ways for many different objects.

Through God (Providence)
3. What role does the Fibonacci Code play in Scripture?

- The Golden Ratio (any number of the code divided by the one before it) is roughly 1.618, and appears in the construction of Noah's Ark and the Ark of the Covenant.

- God employed the Fibonacci Code at creation in the creation of many things, including man, since our DNA molecules take the shape of a double helix spiral following the Code.

4. What role does the Fibonacci Code play in history?

- Leonardo Fibonacci, the Italian mathematician, popularized the sequence in the 13th century.
- Many artists have incorporated the Code into their works, including Van Gogh, Monet, and Whistler.
- The Fibonacci Code is essential to music, as can be best seen on a piano (5 black keys, 8 white keys, 13 keys in an octave, etc.)

For God (Purpose)
5. Does the Fibonacci Code have an eternal purpose?

- It seems likely that God will continue to employ this code in the New Earth, especially since it is a part of human bodies and we know that human bodies will be part of that world.

6. How might we use the Fibonacci Code to further glorify God?

- Some have referred to the Fibonacci Code as God's fingerprint or signature in Creation. We can glorify Him by recognizing this signature and honoring Him for His creative work.
- The Fibonacci Code can be used for apologetics, to point others to God.

The God Grid
(Use this blank grid to give it a try yourself!)

*"For from him and through him and to him are all things.
To him be glory forever. Amen."*
- Romans 11:36

TRIANGLES

From God (Origin)
1. What are some facts about triangles?

_____
_____
_____
_____
_____

2. What do these facts teach us about God who made triangles?

_____
_____
_____
_____
_____

Through God (Providence)
3. What role do triangles play in Scripture?

_____
_____
_____
_____
_____

4. What role do triangles play in history?

_____
_____
_____
_____
_____

For God (Purpose)
5. Do triangles have an eternal purpose?

_____
_____
_____
_____
_____

6. How might we use triangles to further glorify God?

_____
_____
_____
_____
_____

5)

God-Centered Science

"The heavens declare the glory of God,
and the sky above proclaims his handiwork.
Day to day pours out speech,
And night to night reveals knowledge.
- Psalm 19:1-2

In Psalm 19, David rejoices in the two main ways that God has revealed Himself to man. In the first part of the psalm, verses 1-6, he meditates on God's speaking through His creation. He celebrates God's voice in the natural world. Then, in the second part of the psalm, verses 7-11, he celebrates God's voice in Scripture. *"The law of the LORD is perfect, reviving the soul; the testimony of the LORD is sure, making wise the simple"* (v. 7). Here in one psalm we are taught to hear from our God through both *general revelation* and *special revelation*. At the end of the psalm, verses 12-14, we learn what David hoped to gain from God's speech: personal holiness.

Keep back your servant also from presumptuous sins;
  let them not have dominion over me!
Then I shall be blameless,
  and innocent of great transgression.
Let the words of my mouth and the meditation of my heart
  be acceptable in your sight,
  O LORD, my rock and my redeemer"

(vv.13-14)

Just as we seek to grow in faith, love, and purity by hearing from God in His Word, so we should seek to grow by hearing from God in His creation. This should be an aim for our own lives first, but also a skill we seek to give our children. God is speaking all around them, everywhere, in everything He created. Can they hear what He is saying?

Grace will be needed. The first chapter of Romans teaches us that people by nature seek to suppress the truths that creation is teaching them about God. This means these divine truths that we are helping our children to learn from the natural world will not ultimately be embraced by their young hearts unless God by His Holy Spirit intervenes to bless our efforts and to make the hearts of our children receptive. This is a reminder that all of our homeschooling should be accompanied by prayer.

Once our children have begun to know and enjoy God, they can find great delight in seeing God's truth all around them. Our desire should be that they become *Psalm 104 Christians*. Psalm 104 Christians are those who imitate the psalmist in seeing another reason to praise God everywhere they look. As they call to mind various parts of the created world, their hearts are moved to worship.

Here is an exercise that I have found helpful. Read Psalm 104 in the following pages. Notice that the psalm begins with the writer calling on his own soul to bless God. Then, using a pencil or highlighter, note each part of the natural world that the Psalmist brings to his own mind in order to spur his heart on in worship. As you do so, worship along with the psalmist.

¹Bless the LORD, O my soul!
  O LORD my God, you are very great!
You are clothed with splendor and majesty,
² covering yourself with light as with a garment,
  stretching out the heavens like a tent.
³ He lays the beams of his chambers on the waters;
he makes the clouds his chariot;
  he rides on the wings of the wind;
⁴ he makes his messengers winds,
  his ministers a flaming fire.

⁵ He set the earth on its foundations,
  so that it should never be moved.
⁶ You covered it with the deep as with a garment;
  the waters stood above the mountains.
⁷ At your rebuke they fled;
  at the sound of your thunder they took to flight.

⁸ The mountains rose, the valleys sank down
  to the place that you appointed for them.
⁹ You set a boundary that they may not pass,
  so that they might not again cover the earth.

¹⁰ You make springs gush forth in the valleys;
  they flow between the hills;
¹¹ they give drink to every beast of the field;
  the wild donkeys quench their thirst.
¹² Beside them the birds of the heavens dwell;
  they sing among the branches.
¹³ From your lofty abode you water the mountains;
  the earth is satisfied with the fruit of your work.

¹⁴ You cause the grass to grow for the livestock
  and plants for man to cultivate,
that he may bring forth food from the earth
¹⁵   and wine to gladden the heart of man,
oil to make his face shine
  and bread to strengthen man's heart.

¹⁶ The trees of the LORD are watered abundantly,
  the cedars of Lebanon that he planted.
¹⁷ In them the birds build their nests;
  the stork has her home in the fir trees.
¹⁸ The high mountains are for the wild goats;
  the rocks are a refuge for the rock badgers.

¹⁹ He made the moon to mark the seasons;
  the sun knows its time for setting.
²⁰ You make darkness, and it is night,
  when all the beasts of the forest creep about.
²¹ The young lions roar for their prey,
  seeking their food from God.
²² When the sun rises, they steal away
  and lie down in their dens.
²³ Man goes out to his work
  and to his labor until the evening.

²⁴ O LORD, how manifold are your works!
  In wisdom have you made them all;
  the earth is full of your creatures.
²⁵ Here is the sea, great and wide,
  which teems with creatures innumerable,
  living things both small and great.
²⁶ There go the ships,
  and Leviathan, which you formed to play in it.

²⁷ These all look to you,
  to give them their food in due season.
²⁸ When you give it to them, they gather it up;
  when you open your hand, they are filled with good things.
²⁹ When you hide your face, they are dismayed;
  when you take away their breath, they die
  and return to their dust.
³⁰ When you send forth your Spirit, they are created,
  and you renew the face of the ground.

³¹ May the glory of the LORD endure forever;
  may the LORD rejoice in his works,
³² who looks on the earth and it trembles,
  who touches the mountains and they smoke!
³³ I will sing to the LORD as long as I live;
  I will sing praise to my God while I have being.
³⁴ May my meditation be pleasing to him,
  for I rejoice in the LORD.
³⁵ Let sinners be consumed from the earth,
  and let the wicked be no more!
Bless the LORD, O my soul!
Praise the LORD!

The Checkered Coat
Like the author of Psalm 104, early American theologian and pastor
Jonathan Edwards had a keen eye for seeing God's glory in the natural
world. He would take scraps of parchment with him when he went on
his daily horse rides. As insights came to him, he would write them on

the parchment and then pin the scrap to his coat. His biographers tell us that often by the time he returned home it appeared he was wearing a checkered coat because of all the scraps he had pinned to himself.

Many of the insights Edwards gleaned on those daily rides were sparked by what he saw in the natural world around him. He recorded several hundred of these in a work entitle *Images and Shadows of Divine Things*. It is a fascinating read, and good for the soul. Here are just a few examples of his insights:

Roses grow upon briers, which is to signify that all temporal sweets are mixed with bitter. But what seems more especially to be meant by it, is that true happiness, the crown of glory, is to be come at in no other way than by bearing Christ's cross by a life of mortification, self-denial and labor, and bearing all things for Christ. The rose, the chief of all flowers, is the last thing that comes out. The briery prickly bush grows before, but the end and crown of all is the beautiful and fragrant rose.

The serpent's charming of birds and other animals into their mouths, and the spider's taking of the fly in his snare, are lively representations of the devil's catching our souls by his temptations.

The gradual progress we make from childhood to manhood is a type of the gradual progress of the saints in grace.

Tis a sign that the beautiful variety of the colors of light was designed as a type of the various beauties and graces of the Spirit of God.

Ravens that with delight feed on the carrion seem to be remarkable types of devils who with delight prey upon the souls of the dead.

Hills and mountains, as they represent heaven, so they represent eminence in general, or any excellent and high attainment. And as hills, especially high mountains, are not ascended without difficulty and labor, and many rocks and steep places are in the way, so men don't attain to anything eminent or of peculiar excellence without difficulty.

Lightning more commonly strikes high things such as high towers, spires and pinnacles, and high trees, and is observed to be more terrible in mountainous places; which may signify that heaven is an enemy to all proud persons, and that especially makes such the marks of his vengeance.

The beams of the sun can't be scattered, nor the constant stream of their light in the least interrupted or disturbed, by the most violent winds here below; which is a lively image of what is true concerning heavenly light, communicated from Christ, the Sun of Righteousness to the soul. 'Tis not in the power of the storms and changes of the world to destroy that light and comfort; yea, death itself can have no hold of it. The reasons why the sun's light is not disturbed by winds is two-fold: first, the light is of so pure and subtle a nature that that which is so gross as the wind can have no hold of it; and second, the sun, the luminary, is far above, out of the reach of winds. These things are lively images of what is spiritual.

Over the last several years, I have had the opportunity to teach homeschool students about Jonathan Edwards and his eye for God's glory in nature. I especially enjoy taking students outside, equipped with notebooks and pencils, and urging them to spend some time walking around alone, observing. As they look upon the sky, plants, insects, and animals, I urge them to see the metaphors that God has interwoven into our world to teach us spiritual truths. Once we gather back together and share our insights, the experience is truly worshipful and encouraging to our souls.

Homeschool families might consider guiding their children to keep their own nature journal, much like Edwards'. They can draw their observations from nature hikes, label various parts of the plants or animals they saw, record their identifications, but also jot down *spiritual* insights they discover as they observe the natural world.

Science Is from God

As we think about applying the God Grid to science, it should first be noted that all of the truths we discovered about *mathematical* principles in the last chapter apply equally to *scientific* principles. In the last chapter we used the equation 5+5=10 and observed that it is true, eternal, omnipresent, transcendent, etc. All of those same observations can be accurately made about any scientific law. In his book *Redeeming Science,* Vern Poythress says:

> It suffices to observe that, in reality, what people call "scientific law" is divine. We are speaking of God himself and his revelation of himself through his governance of the world. Scientists must believe in scientific law in order to carry out their work. When we analyze what this scientific law really is, we find that scientists are constantly confronted with God himself, the Trinitarian God, and are constantly depending on who he is and what he does in conformity with his divine nature. In thinking about law, scientists are thinking God's thoughts after him.[7]

Let us practice using the God Grid on the scientific principle of *heliocentrism.* This is the fact that the *sun* is the center of our solar system, and that the planets (including earth) revolve around the sun. This fact has prevailed over the false notion of *geocentrism,* the idea that the sun and planets revolve around the earth.

Most students will study heliocentrism multiple times in their homeschooling. They may first learn the principle when they are young and mom helps them construct a model of the solar system. They may learn it again as preteens while doing a report on Nicolaus Copernicus. They will likely go deeper into the subject once they are high school age and study physical science. At all of these levels students can apply the God Grid, their answers maturing along with their own knowledge and understanding. I recently had the joy of leading a group of homeschool students in this discussion, and their answers (some of which are expressed below) displayed splendid insight and led us into a greater sense of wonder towards God.

First, what are some basic facts about heliocentrism? Here are a few possibilities that your children might mention:

- The earth revolves around the sun.
- The sun is the center of our solar system.
- The sun makes life on earth possible.
- The earth is positioned perfectly in relation to the sun for the sustaining of life.

Now, what can we learn from these facts about our God? Very likely, your children will be quick to see the metaphor our God has woven into our world. The sun seems to represent Him. Like the sun, God is the center of all things. His existence does not revolve around us, but ours revolves around Him. Just as people had to change their thinking when they discovered that the solar system revolved around the sun and not the earth, so we must adjust ours to realize that this world is ultimately about God, and not us.

The metaphor continues with the sun's relation to earth. Just as the sun provides life on earth, so it is God who ultimately makes all life possible. Jesus is the *light of the world* (John 8:12), and therefore, the *Author of life* (Acts 3:15).

One homeschool student recalled the following C. S. Lewis quote while we were having this discussion. Lewis said, "I believe in Christianity as I believe that the sun has risen, not only because I see it but because by it I see everything else." The student suggested that just as we are able to see through the light of the sun, so ultimately it is through God's light – His Word – that we can see things as they actually are and walk in the way of blessing. *"Your word is a lamp to my feet and a light to my path"* (Psalm 119:105). *"For with you is the fountain of life; in your light do we see light"* (Psalm 36:9).

It should be noted here that these homeschool students were not yet thinking about the role of heliocentrism in the Bible, but only the truths they could learn from the scientific facts on this subject. However, like the Psalm 104 Christian described before, they were quick to see *spiritual* truths in *physical* realities. This is a key mark of having a truly God-centered worldview, and an important goal that we should have for our children.

Perhaps it should also be added here that ultimately it is *special* revelation (the Bible) that trumps our understanding of spiritual truths from *natural* revelation (Creation). Therefore, we should always test our spiritual conclusions on the basis of Scripture. For example, if our children observe that science tells us that one day our sun will die out, and draw from that fact the conclusion that one day God will cease to exist as well, we must surely correct them. The lessons God is teaching us through nature are always in accordance with His Word, and any idea that contradicts that Word must be rejected.

Added to seeing a metaphor for God-centeredness in the way He established our solar system, your children might note attributes of God related to the sun. Certainly, we see God's care for us, since He established the earth in such relation to the sun that we would exist and be provided for. They might also mention His power, His wisdom, His goodness, and more.

Science Is through God
Having considered with our children what we can learn about God as the One who ordained and established heliocentrism, we can now think on the role of this truth in Scripture and history. We are leading our children in considering this truth in God's providence.

Thinking about Scripture, students may point to Bible stories that speak of the sun acting abnormally. My students thought immediately of the sun standing still in the sky for Joshua and the Israelites (Joshua 10:13), as well as moving backwards in the sky for Hezekiah (Isaiah 38:8). Their observation was that though these events were described from the perspective of people on the earth's surface, what God actually did was pause/turn back the rotation of the earth. The sun remained as it had been before. Similarly, God always remains the same and does not change, but He regularly acts upon the lives of people in ways both seen and unseen.

Another miracle my students mentioned was the darkening of the sun in Exodus 10, where there was no light in all of Egypt except for in Goshen, where the Israelites dwelt. This reveals God's power over the sun in its relationship to earth. Some suggest God used clouds to perform this miracle, but the darkness is described in the passage as *pitch* darkness, "*a darkness to be felt.*" How do we explain this? In Genesis 1, God created light *before* He created the sun. It is not the sun that is the ultimate source of light, but God Himself. The sun is merely a tool which God uses. God can easily bring light or withhold light upon any place as He pleases. Here we see His sovereignty and supremacy in the world.

What about the role heliocentrism has played in history? Obviously it is integral to history itself – there would be no history without it! Your children might also speak of those whose scientific contributions involved the principle of heliocentrism, men such as Copernicus and Johannes Kepler. The geocentrism/heliocentrism debate of the 16th and 17th centuries impacted the lives of many, especially in Europe, and men such as Galileo were condemned by the Roman Catholic Church and imprisoned for rejecting the geocentric view.

Let me remind you here that younger children will likely know very little about the role of heliocentrism in history. This will be true about many subjects. You as a parent can guide younger ones in these conversations with your own knowledge, while looking forward to the days ahead when your children will be able to go deeper with you. The more books they read, the more facts they memorize while they are young, and the more dialectic their thinking becomes as they mature, the richer and better these conversations will become.

Science Is for God

Does heliocentrism have an *eternal* purpose, or merely a temporal one? Certainly, the spiritual truth taught by heliocentrism will remain forever true. God is the One from Whom and through Whom and for Whom all exists, and this will be true in the next age as well as this one.

Your children might recall the end of the Bible, where the New Jerusalem (the eternal heaven) is described this way:

> *And the city has no need of sun or moon to shine on it, for the glory of God gives it light, and its lamp is the Lamb. By its light will the nations walk, and the kings of the earth will bring their glory into it, and its gates will never be shut by day—and there will be no night there.* - Revelation 21:23-25

There is mystery here, and Christians debate whether this passage should be interpreted literally or figuratively. Taken literally, it appears that the principle of heliocentrism will continue into eternity, but not with the star we call our *sun* at the center, but God Himself. As He has always been, He will continue to be our light and our life, the source and sustenance and purpose of our very being.

How can we use the scientific truth of heliocentrism to glorify God? My students discussed *humility*, and how this truth should lead us to place God above our own selves in our allegiance and love. This truth can also be used as an illustration to teach the spiritual truth of God—centeredness to others. Every time children work on creating a model of the solar system, we have the opportunity to talk with them about the supreme worth of our God.

Helps for God-Centered Science
Let me remind you that the God Grid is simply one tool to help you lead your children in discovering God's wisdom and glory in the various subjects they study. Do not feel that you are constrained by the questions on the grid, or somehow obligated to answer them all. One of the beauties of having these conversations is that we do not always know where they are going to go, and it is often in the midst of the conversation that God brings to mind questions that can take our children a step further into God-glorifying thoughts about the subject at hand. Let the grid be a tool in your toolbox, but don't hesitate to pose other questions to your children that you think will be helpful.

As with the study of math, I encourage you to supplement your science curriculum with books and resources that connect the principles of science to history and real people. The history of science is filled with interesting people and reveal God's mysterious ways of bringing about unexpected and fascinating discoveries.

Here are a few recommended resources:

- *Redeeming Science: A God-Centered Approach* by Vern Poythress.
- *The Language of God: A Scientist Presents Evidence for Belief* by Francis Collins.
- *100 Scientists Who Shaped World History* by John Tiner.
- *Notable Notebooks: Scientists and Their Writings* by Jessica Fries-Gaither.
- The *Living History Library* biographies of scientists by Jeanne Bendick.

The God Grid
(Sample from homeschool students[4])

"For from him and through him and to him are all things.
To him be glory forever. Amen."
- Romans 11:36

THE ATMOSPHERE

From God (Origin)
1. What are some facts about the atmosphere?

- The atmosphere is made up of a mixture of gases (especially Nitrogen and Oxygen) which surround the earth.
- Gravity holds our atmosphere in place, allowing us to live and breathe.
- The layer of atmosphere filled with ozone gas protects us from the sun.
- The atmosphere sustains our planet at a moderate, livable temperature-range.

2. What do these facts teach us about God who made the atmosphere?

- God must be powerful to have created the atmosphere.
- God must be wise to have designed the atmosphere.
- God must be loving to give us the atmosphere for our life and protection.
- Just as we need the atmosphere between us and the sun in order to have its light without dying, so we need a Mediator between us and God so that we can have a relationship with Him without being destroyed (because of our sin.)

Through God (Providence)

3. What role does the atmosphere play in Scripture?

- Based on the ages people reached in the book of Genesis, and that there was no rain failing from the sky until Noah's flood, the atmosphere must have been different at that period of history than it is now. Some believe that a dense layer of moisture surrounded the earth, lessening the sun's destructive influence (allowing people to live longer), and that the destruction of this layer was the means of the Great Flood.

4. What role does the atmosphere play in history?

- People have been studying the atmosphere for a long time, especially as relates to climate and weather. Times of drought, famine, flooding, and other atmosphere-related events have shaped human history.
- The debate over climate change, global warming, and the condition of the ozone layer has been a hot topic for many decades.

For God (Purpose)

5. Does the atmosphere have an eternal purpose?

- It seems likely that the New Earth will continue to have an atmosphere, especially since people will still have physical bodies.

6. How might we use the atmosphere to further glorify God?

- We should be grateful to God for the atmosphere.
- We should honor God by being faithful caretakers of the atmosphere He has given us.

The God Grid
(Sample from homeschool students[4])

"For from him and through him and to him are all things.
To him be glory forever. Amen."
- Romans 11:36

FIRE

From God (Origin)
1. What are some facts about fire?

- Fire provides warmth and light.
- Fire can be harmful when not properly used and contained.
- Fire cannot last without fuel.

2. What do these facts teach us about God who made fire?

- God is a Provider; the gift of fire has sustained life, provided many comforts, and propelled the development of cultures.
- God intends for His gifts to be used rightly; fire reminds us that the misuse of God's gifts can do us great harm.
- Just as fire requires fuel to endure, so the fire of our faith requires fuel: God's Word, prayer, Christian fellowship, etc.

Through God (Providence)
3. What role does fire play in Scripture?

- God appeared in fire at the burning bush and at Mount Sinai.
- Israel was commanded to offer burnt offerings to God.
- Shadrach, Meshach, and Abednego were thrown into a furnace of fire because of their faith.
- God is called "a consuming fire" in Hebrews 12:29, and we are therefore told to offer Him "acceptable worship, with reverence and awe."

- Throughout Scripture, and especially in the gospels and Revelation, hell is described as a place of fire.

4. What role does fire play in history?

- Fire has been essential to the development of every culture.
- Fire was used to alert people of danger along the Great Wall of China.
- Fire was used in lighthouses to guide ships away from danger.
- Fire has been used in war, including on arrows used to burn enemy encampments and villages.
- Burning coal continues to sustain electricity for many people around the world.

For God (Purpose)
5. Does fire have an eternal purpose?

- Some Christians believe that hell really is a pit of fire in which unbelievers will forever suffer; others believe it is a metaphor used to make hell more intelligible to us. If we take the literal approach, it seems likely fire will continue as an instrument of God's judgment.

6. How might we use fire to further glorify God?

- When we think about the many conveniences we have through fire, or sit by a fireplace on a winter's night, we should thank God for this great gift.
- We can use fire to serve others and meet their needs.
- Fire can be used to honor God as stewards of His earth, such as when Park Rangers use controlled burns.

The God Grid
(Sample from homeschool students[4])

*"For from him and through him and to him are all things.
To him be glory forever. Amen."*
- Romans 11:36

OXYGEN

From God (Origin)
1. What are some facts about oxygen?

- We are dependent on oxygen for life.
- Oxygen is part of the composition of air.
- Oxygen is found all over the earth.
- Some compounds that include oxygen are toxic.

2. What do these facts teach us about God who made oxygen?

- God's care is displayed in His provision of oxygen for us.
- That God made us dependent on oxygen ultimately teaches us our dependence on Him for life and well-being.
- God's creation of oxygen reveals that His sovereignty extends beyond the world we can see to the microscopic realm.
- God's use of oxygen in various compounds reveals His fondness for sense and order in the makeup of His universe.

Through God (Providence)
3. What role does oxygen play in Scripture?

- Oxygen was a part of Creation.
- Wherever people are breathing in the Bible, the oxygen God provides is present.
- It was God who breathed into Adam the breath of life, making Him a living being.

- Oxygen is part of the composition of water, so wherever water appears in Scripture, oxygen is present.

4. What role does oxygen play in history?

- Oxygen is essential to history in its sustenance of life, its inclusion in our atmosphere, in the makeup of water, etc.
- Joseph Priestley is credited with discovering oxygen as a distinct element in 1774.
- Oxygen as part of combustion was essential to the invention of engines.
- Oxygen has been used for many military purposes, including fuel-air bombs.

For God (Purpose)
5. Does oxygen have an eternal purpose?

- Probably. We do not know if the atmosphere of heaven will be composed of oxygen, or if our human bodies will still need oxygen in heaven, but it is likely. Revelation speaks of water when describing heaven, which would include oxygen.

6. How might we use oxygen to further glorify God?

- We should thank God for the oxygen He gives us to live.
- We should be humbled by our dependence on God and remembering how frail we really are.
- We should seek to make our every breath count for the glory of God.

The God Grid
(Use this blank grid to give it a try yourself!)

*"For from him and through him and to him are all things.
To him be glory forever. Amen."*
- Romans 11:36

THE DIGESTIVE SYSTEM

From God (Origin)
1. What are some facts about the digestive system?

_____
_____
_____
_____
_____

2. What do these facts teach us about God who made the digestive system?

_____
_____
_____
_____
_____

Through God (Providence)
3. What role does the digestive system play in Scripture?

_____
_____
_____
_____
_____

4. What role does the digestive system play in history?

_____
_____
_____
_____
_____

For God (Purpose)
5. Does the digestive system have an eternal purpose?

_____
_____
_____
_____
_____

6. How might we use the digestive system to further glorify God?

_____
_____
_____
_____
_____

6)

God-Centered Language and Literature

"In the beginning was the Word,
and the Word was with God,
and the Word was God."
- John 1:1

Words matter. God created human beings to be a people of speech, and our use of language to communicate is an essential part of our humanness. Whatever God calls our children to be or do in the future, we can be sure of this: they will be *talkers*. They will be people who communicate (eloquently or poorly) through speech and writing. They will influence others for good or ill through language. They will be influenced by the words of others. Our lives are molded and shaped through communication, and this is bound up in our nature because we are image-bearers of God. Consider these words from author Paul Tripp:

> You do not really understand the significance of words until you realize that the first words that human ears ever heard were not the words of another human being, but the words of God! The value of every piece of human communications is rooted in the fact that *God* speaks. Into the sights and sounds of the newly created world came the voice of God, speaking words of human language to Adam and Eve. When God chose to reveal himself that way, he raised talk to a place of highest significance as his primary vehicle of truth. Through words, we would come to know the most important truths that could be known – truths that reveal God's existence and glory, truths that give life.[8]

The moment we begin teaching our children the alphabet, we are preparing them for a life rich in language. They are participants in a divine activity. Within the Trinity there is communication between the persons of the Godhead (cf. Psalm 2:1; John 15:15). In history, God speaks to man, and man speaks back to God. Human beings speak to each other, and sometimes, we even speak to ourselves! Our goal in teaching our children language should be higher than the mere mastery of grammatical principles. Our goal should be that our children would see the glory of God in the parts of speech, in the steps of a persuasive argument, in the vast varieties and types of languages in the world. We want to equip our children to use language well *for* the glory of God, but we also want them to *behold* the glory of God in language itself.

Thankful for Verbs

One very practical way of doing this is to take any particular aspect of language study and ask the question: "Why should we be thankful for this?" For example, "Why should we be thankful for *verbs*?" I asked this question recently to a group of homeschool students of varying ages who were working with Latin verbs, and were perhaps tempted to *not* be thankful! The discussion wound up being about our *favorite* verbs – the ones we would miss most if those actions no longer existed. One student said he was thankful for the verb *laugh*, and we thought for a moment about a world without laughter. Another student said she was grateful for the verb *sing*, and the whole group agreed. Other verbs mentioned included *smile, ponder, read, see, listen, eat*, and of course, *love*. One thoughtful student pointed out all that would be lost if the verb *play* did not exist - no *playing* music, *playing* sports, *playing* board games, *playing* video games, and no *playing* with toys. A world without the verb *play* would be a much more dismal world to live in.

Underneath all of these other verbs is the most important verb of all – the one that makes all others possible: *I AM*. Our God's divine name is made up of the verb *to be*. It is only because He *is* that you and I *are*. It is only because He is that we can be and do so many different verbs. *I AM* is the beginning, middle, and end of all verbs, and every verb ultimately exists for the *I AM*. Whatever activities we enjoy, be they laughing, smiling, playing, or loving, they should lead us to praise the God from whom all these blessings flow.

What is wonderful about a discussion like this is that we can easily have similar ones with our children using almost any of the elements of language. If our children are struggling with gerunds, or the right use of commas, or the requirements for a true sentence, we can pause from the lesson and encourage their hearts by having a *thankfulness* discussion concerning the subject at hand.

Glorious Conjunctions

Another way to help our children see God's good purposes in language is to connect the grammar they are learning to Scripture. For example, we might assign our kids a "scavenger hunt" through the Bible to try and spot imperatives or compound-complex sentences. For our older children, we might encourage them to look through the Bible or draw upon their Scripture memory to list a number of verses where adjectives or adverbs are particularly important and glorious. For example, John 3:16 says that those who believe on Jesus are given *eternal* life. What a wonderful adjective to our ears!

One of my favorite discussions to have with students is about conjunctions. The Bible is full of little conjunctions bearing the weight of heavy glory. Consider these words from Ephesians 2:1-3:

And you were dead in the trespasses and sins in which you once walked, following the course of this world, following the prince of the power of the air, the spirit that is now at work in the sons of disobedience — among whom we all once lived in the passions of our flesh, carrying out the desires of the body and the mind, and were by nature children of wrath, like the rest of mankind.

This passage presents a depressing assessment of mankind. These verses are not describing Christians who have been saved by God's grace, but natural human beings – who we are apart from Jesus. We are described here are as the walking dead, living in spiritual deadness because of our sins. We are described here as worldly, following the ways of the world. We are followers of the devil himself, children of the devil, walking in his ways of disobedience. Natural man is directed not by God's will, but by his own passions, fulfilling his own selfish desires. What is the result of all this? We are by nature children of *wrath*. We deserve the judgment of God. We deserve an eternal punishment.

If Paul stopped there, we would be left in utter despair. There would be no hope for us. Hell would be our inevitable, eternal destination. But

Paul does not stop there. He continues, and his next word is a glorious conjunction: *but*.

Yes, we are by nature spiritually dead. Yes, we are by nature worldly, followers of the devil, slaves to our own fleshly desires, deserving of God's wrath. BUT! Despite all that!

> *But God, being rich in mercy, because of the great love with which he loved us, even when we were dead in our trespasses, made us alive together with Christ—by grace you have been saved — and raised us up with him and seated us with him in the heavenly places in Christ Jesus, so that in the coming ages he might show the immeasurable riches of his grace in kindness toward us in Christ Jesus.*
>
> *– Ephesians 2:4-6*

Do you see how glorious one little conjunction can be? In that one conjunction, even before the glorious truths that follow, we learn that all of our sin and guilt were not enough to hinder the purpose of God to do us good. That word *but* means *hope* for us!

Pastor D. Martyn Lloyd-Jones once famously preached an entire sermon on the two words *"But God... "* He ended by saying,

> [This] is what the Christian message, the Christian faith has to say to this wretched, distracted, unhappy, confused, frustrated, modern world...It is all the outcome of these essential doctrines which can be learned only in this Book which is God's Word. [This] is the world! – "But God..."[9]

What a joy it can be to help our children connect the principles they are learning in language study to the thrilling truths of God's Word.

Diagramming Scripture
Related to the previous discussion, another beneficial way to connect our children's study of grammar to God is by having our children diagram Scripture. The practice of diagramming sentences has fallen out of favor in most public schools, but is thankfully being recovered and preserved among many homeschoolers. The benefits of diagramming sentences include:

- Helping students truly understand the functions of the various parts of speech and how they work together
- Training students' brains to think logically in connecting words and phrases into arguments
- Teaching students how to exposit a text in order to determine an author's intended meaning
- Equipping students to spot errors in weak sentences in order to improve them

Over the last decade, I have enjoyed leading many homeschool students in diagramming sentences from important documents such as the *Declaration of Independence* and the *U.S. Constitution*. Yet no document is worthier of the time and attention to a text that diagramming brings than the Bible. In particular, diagramming can help students follow many of the Apostle Paul's long sentences, revealing how the various propositions he connects together deliver a forceful and cohesive argument. It also helps students distinguish main points from supporting or subordinate points. I always love it when students show me their notes from diagramming their pastor's sermon text during a Sunday service. This is such a valuable practice for their minds and hearts, and may even put a little pressure on their pastors to stay faithful in sticking to the text!

If diagramming sentences is new to you, I recommend Nancy Wilson's *Our Mother Tongue: A Guide to English Grammar* as a great place to start. If there is a Classical Conversations® community in your area, participating in their Essentials program can reap great rewards in this regard.

The Skill of Exposition
As a pastor, I wish all the members of the church I serve were skilled in exposition. It would make my job a great deal easier.

Have you ever been in a small group Bible study, perhaps studying one of the epistles? The leader reads a verse aloud and then asks for discussion. One person responds, "When I hear that verse, I like to think it means..." Another chimes in, "Here is what it means to me..." One by one, far too often, people will read their own opinions and ideas into the text. Instead of looking at the actual words the author uses, the grammar, punctuation, and context, they allow the feelings and ideas that sprung up as they heard the verse read to dictate its meaning. Instead of discerning what the *author* intends to say, they give the verse their own meaning, one usually produced by the connotations the employed words have formed in their minds throughout their life experiences. The result is the *opposite* of exposition: they bring their own meaning to the text instead of pulling the author's meaning out. This is how much error and false teaching continue to hold sway in people's lives, even as they are supposedly "studying the Bible."

As parents, we want our children to learn the skill of discerning an author's intended meaning in whatever text they are reading. This will serve them well throughout their years, whether they are reading an email, a policy manual at their workplace, a letter from a dear friend, or the very Word of God. This skill can only be learned as you and your child interact over sentences, paragraphs, and chapters, discussing together the ideas being conveyed. It is not enough for our children to tell us *what* they believe an author is saying; they must be able to show us in the text *why* they have that interpretation. This is true for novels as well as for nonfiction writing.

As an example, consider the following passage from Elizabeth George Speare's excellent children's novel *The Sign of the Beaver*.

> An uncomfortable doubt had long been troubling Matt. Now, before Attean went away, he had to know. "This land," he said slowly, "this place where my father built his cabin. Did it belong to your grandfather? Did he own it once?"
>
> "How one man own ground?" Attean questioned.
>
> "Well, my father owns it now. He bought it."
>
> "I not understand." Attean scowled. "How can man own land? Land same as air. Land for all people to live on. For beaver and deer. Does deer own land?"
>
> How could you explain, Matt wondered, to someone who did not want to understand? Somewhere in the back of his mind, there was a sudden suspicion that Attean was making sense and he was not.[10]

After reading this passage with our children, we might ask, "What do you think Elizabeth George Speare is saying in this paragraph?" This is a dialectic exercise, better fitting the development of children over age ten. These older children might struggle at first to separate in their minds what the *characters* are saying from what the *author* is saying. Yet through the characters, the author speaks. If our children are to practice discernment as they read fiction throughout their lives, they must learn to see through the words of the characters to the intention of the author.

In discussing this passage with homeschool students, I have often pointed out that Matt and Attean are coming at the issue of private property from two different perspectives. Matt is coming from a worldview that approves of land ownership and private property, whereas Attean is coming from a worldview that rejects the very concept. Then I ask this question: based on this passage, which view does the *author* seem to favor? Astute students point to the last sentence in the quoted passage. There, Mrs. Speare seems to show her hand, hinting that Matt's view is in the wrong. The reader, consciously or not, is left with the impression that Attean's view is the stronger one. This is exposition – pulling the author's ideas from the text.

We must not stop at exposition, however. Once our children have identified an idea that an author is teaching, we must lead them to *assess* that idea in light of Scripture. This is where God Grids can be applied to literature.

From God

We begin by teaching our children to choose a single proposition from a book they are reading. All good novels are conveyors of an author's ideas, put into literary form, in order to invoke a response in the reader. Our children should seek to discover one of these ideas, and assess it biblically.

For practice, let's use a rather simple example. In Harper Lee's novel *To Kill a Mockingbird*, there is a powerful courtroom scene in which the main character's father (Atticus Finch) defends a black man against a false accusation. As she watches from the courtroom balcony with the people of color, her father risks his reputation and welfare in that prejudiced Alabama community by giving the man a strong defense. It is a heroic moment. After the trial, as Atticus is leaving the courtroom, one of the men in the balcony says, "Miss Jean Louise, stand up. Your father's passin'." Together, the men and women of color, joined by Atticus' daughter, honor him by standing as he exits.[11]

95

One idea we might draw from that passage is that it is right to give honor to those to whom honor is due. The author presents this as a lesson learned by the main character, but the reader is learning the lesson right along with her. However, rather than accepting this lesson blindly, we must assess that truth. Do we agree with it? As Christians, coming from a biblical perspective, can we affirm this truth? In this case we certainly can, and so we are able to move forward with our God Grid. We place this proposition as the answer to our first question, and move on to the second (see the examples at the end of this chapter).

What can we learn about God from the truth that it is right to give honor to those to whom honor is due? Your children might suggest many ideas. One of my students observed that God Himself is honorable, and is the Maker of all things honorable, and thus to honor the good in others is to honor Him. When we honor those who have acted in some virtuous way, we are honoring the very character of God displayed in them. Your children might also observe that this truth reveals that God loves all that is good and right, and seeks to lift up the good and the right before our eyes. Certainly, our families and local churches should be places where we learn to love what is good as those around us honor the godliness they see in one another.

What if the author's idea is *wrong*? What if your student correctly identifies an idea an author is communicating, but it is an idea that the Bible declares is wrong? In that case, we must reject the author's proposition and replace it with a true one. For example, in the case of our passage from *The Sign of the Beaver,* we saw that the author seemed to be suggesting that it is wrong for people to own property. As a Christian parent seeking to train up my children in a biblical worldview, I would urge them to reject that proposition. The Bible has much to say about the goodness of private property, and the eighth commandment ("You shall not steal") implies the sanctity of private ownership. For our God Grid, we would replace the false proposition with a true one: "It is right for people to own private property." We could then continue with the Grid from there, focusing on our true proposition.

Through God

Let's go back to the proposition that it is right to give honor to those to whom honor is due. We ask our children, "Where do we see this in Scripture?" They could give many answers, possibly including:

- Abraham's offering to Melchizedek (Genesis 14:20)
- The fifth commandment (Exodus 20:12)
- The leper who returned to Jesus to give thanks (Luke 17:11-19)
- The command to honor the elderly (Leviticus 19:32)
- The command to honor our church leaders (1 Timothy 5:17)
- Heaven resounds with honor for God (Revelation 4:11)
- The last day, when those who should have been honored for their godliness in this life but were not will be honored by God Himself. *"The last will be first, and the first last"* (Matthew 20:16).

In having this discussion with my own sons, they thought of Mark 12:17: *"Render to Caesar the things that are Caesars..."* The conversation took an unexpected turn as we talked about submitting to God-appointed authorities, paying taxes, and showing honor to a person's *office* even when the one filling that office is dishonorable.

Where do we see this principle in history? The desire to show honor to those deemed worthy has been woven into the hearts of men. Every tribe of people in every generation has sought to pay tribute to their great ones. The possible answers are innumerable. Some include:

- Days set aside to show honor, such as Memorial Day, Mother's Day, or Veterans Day
- Ceremonies intended to show honor, ranging from small local events to Presidential inaugurations
- Biographies written to help future generations remember the contributions of individuals in the past
- Many songs and poems have been written as tributes to honor the feats of notable men and women, from ancient times to today.

For God

Does this principle have an eternal purpose? Certainly! For all eternity, God's people will give Him honor and glory. He is the One worthy of supreme honor, the One who defines what is truly *honorable.*

> *And I heard every creature in heaven and on earth and under the earth and in the sea, and all that is in them, saying, "To him who sits on the throne and to the Lamb be blessing and honor and glory and might forever and ever!"* (Revelation 5:13)

How can we use this purpose to glorify God? Every time we show honor to someone to whom it is due, we honor God Himself. He is the Giver of all good things. When we honor our parents, we are honoring God's gift to us. When we honor those around us for their good qualities, we are honoring that which is godly in them. We are exalting His character and His attributes. God is seen to be great as we count others more significant than ourselves (Philippians 2:3), and as we outdo one another in showing honor (Romans 12:10). Only the power of God can change self-centered hearts so that they are willing to put others first in this way. The power of His gospel to transform lives is seen in our honoring of others.

Helps for God-Centered Language and Literature

Remember, using the God Grid is only one way that we can help our students see the glory of God in their study of literature. This method brings together the skills of exposition, critical thinking, and rhetoric, while drawing upon their knowledge of Scripture and history. By integrating skills and subjects, our children see the wisdom of God in the complexity and beauty of this world, and protects them against a false isolation of subjects (as if novels exist in a vacuum). Also, this method focuses on the novel itself at the step of *exposition*, but ultimately leaves it behind to focus on the proposition being conveyed. This helps our children see that art does not exist for its own sake, but finds its value in the service of truth.

Here are a few recommended resources:

- *In the Beginning Was the Word: Language - A God-Centered Approach* by Vern Poythress
- *Our Mother Tongue: A Guide to English Grammar* by Nancy Wilson
- *The War Against Grammar* by David Mulroy
- *Echoes of Eden: Reflections on Christianity, Literature, and the Arts* by Jerram Barrs

The God Grid
(Sample from homeschool students[4])

THE SCARLET LETTER

Exposition
What is a proposition being put forward by this author?
Suppressed guilt is the undoing of a man.

Do you agree that this proposition is true?
Yes

TRUTH: Suppressed guilt is the undoing of a man.

From God (Origin)
1. What are some facts about this truth?

- Guilt is the result of sin.
- Guilt makes a person feel bad.
- Guilt can make it difficult for a person to think straight.

2. What does this truth teach us about God?

- God wants us to repent.
- God is against us if we will not confess our sins.
- Guilt is a gift from God to lead us to repentance.

Through God (Providence)
3. What role does this truth play in Scripture?

- Guilt led Judas Iscariot to commit suicide.
- There is a kind of sorrow for sin that leads to repentance, and a kind that leads to death (2nd Corinthians 7:10-11).
- James says that anyone who knows the right thing to do and fails to do it, for him it is sin.

4. What role does this truth play in history?

- Guilt has been a part of everyone's lives since the first humans.
- Many have turned to destructive behaviors, addictions, and even suicide because of guilt.
- President Richard Nixon was made physically sick by his feelings of guilt.
- Criminals have had fatal heart attacks rooted in their unshakable sense of guilt for crimes they committed.

For God (Purpose)
5. Does this truth have an eternal purpose?

- There will be no guilt in heaven, but there will be many in heaven who were driven to Christ by their guilt.
- Those in hell will forever know their guilt before God and will never be able to accuse God of treating them unjustly.

6. How might we use this truth to further glorify God?

- It is right for us to help others sense their guilt for sins they've committed, but only so we might then point them to Jesus as the one who takes away all their guilt.
- We should regularly confess our own sins. James 5:16: "Therefore, confess your sins to one another and pray for one another, that you may be healed."

The God Grid
(Sample from homeschool students[4])

THE CALL OF THE WILD

Exposition
What is a proposition being put forward by this author?
Man is an animal.

Do you agree that this proposition is true?
No

TRUTH: Human beings are distinct from the animals.

From God (Origin)
1. What are some facts about this truth?

- Many people believe humans are mere animals.
- Humans were created in the image of God.
- Humans were given dominion over the animals.

2. What does this truth teach us about God?

- God delights to behold images of Himself.
- God designed for animals to be cared for by humans.
- God has given a proper order to His Creation.

Through God (Providence)
3. What role does this truth play in Scripture?

- God created man after the animals and charged him to care for them.
- Adam gave names to all the animals.
- God did not come as an animal, but as a human, to die for humans.

4. What role does this truth play in history?

- Man has employed many animals for farming, transportation, and as pets.
- Since the Fall, people and animals have often had adversarial relationships.
- Evolutionary theory has blurred the lines between humans and animals, elevating the dignity of animals and demeaning the dignity of humans.
- Some zoos have displayed humans in cages.

For God (Purpose)
5. Does this truth have an eternal purpose?

- Since heaven is described as a New Earth, and books like Isaiah seem to speak of animals in heaven, it is likely that man will continue to be distinct from animals there and entrusted with their care.
- The sin of mistreating animals or treating humans as animals will stand against unbelievers on the Day of Judgment.

6. How might we use this truth to further glorify God?

- Christians should emphasize the many obvious differences between human beings and all other animals.
- Christians should stand up for the dignity of human life.
- Christians should honor God by being good stewards and caretakers of the animal kingdom.

The God Grid
(Sample from homeschool students[4])

THE BEST CHRISTMAS PAGEANT EVER

Exposition
What is a proposition being put forward by this author?
We should not judge people by their outward appearance.

Do you agree that this proposition is true?
Yes

TRUTH: We should not judge people by their outward appearance.

From God (Origin)
1. What are some facts about this truth?

- God has made all people different from one another.
- The outward appearance of a person is not always a good reflection of the inward character of that person.
- We are often tempted to make judgements based on appearances.

2. What does this truth teach us about God?

- God calls us to care more about the inside of a person than the outside.
- God Himself looks at the heart.
- God values virtue over vanity.

Through God (Providence)

3. What role does this truth play in Scripture?

- God appointed David to be King over Israel, declaring that He looks at the heart (1st Samuel 16:7).
- God instructs His people to choose leaders based on character, not appearance (1st Timothy 3).

4. What role does this truth play in history?

- During slavery in the U.S., black-skinned people were seen as inferior because of their outward appearance.
- Many ill-fated marriages were entered into because of attraction to outward beauty rather than inner beauty.

For God (Purpose)

5. Does this truth have an eternal purpose?

- Though our outward bodies in heaven will be glorified and marvelous, it will be the inner beauty of our souls that will most reflect God's glory.
- In heaven, all sinful "judging" will no longer happen.

6. How might we use this truth to further glorify God?

- Like our God, we should be intentional about looking at people's character rather than their outward appearance.
- We should put away all racism and racial prejudice from our lives.
- We should value inner beauty over outer beauty when choosing a spouse.
- We should look for godly character rather than outward attractiveness when choosing leaders.

The God Grid
(Use this blank grid to give it a try yourself!)

THE THREE LITTLE PIGS

Exposition
What is a proposition being put forward by this author?

Do you agree that this proposition is true?

TRUTH: _____

From God (Origin)
1. What are some facts about this truth?

_____
_____
_____
_____
_____

2. What does this truth teach us about God?

_____
_____
_____
_____
_____

Through God (Providence)
3. What role does this truth play in Scripture?

_____
_____
_____
_____
_____

4. What role does this truth play in history?

_____
_____
_____
_____
_____

For God (Purpose)
5. Does this truth have an eternal purpose?

_____
_____
_____
_____
_____

6. How might we use this truth to further glorify God?

_____
_____
_____
_____
_____

7)

God Centered History

"...and he does according to his will
among the host of heaven
and among the inhabitants of the earth;
and none can stay his hand
or say to him, 'What have you done?'"
- Daniel 4:35

The value of studying history is affirmed throughout the Bible. It is nothing less than the study of God's providence – His ways with men. When Ephesians 1:11 says that God *"works all things according to the counsel of his will,"* the implication is that every historical event, no matter how seemingly insignificant, has come about by God's power in accordance with God's plan. Therefore, to study history is to study God.

Admittedly, the higher your view of God's sovereignty, the more God-centered your understanding of history will be. My own view is in alignment with that of Charles Spurgeon, who said,

> "I believe that every particle of dust that dances in the sunbeam does not move an atom more or less than God wishes—that every particle of spray that dashes against the steamboat has its orbit as well as the sun in the heavens—that the chaff from the hand of the winnower is steered as the stars in their courses. The creeping of an aphid over the rosebud is as much fixed as the march of the devastating pestilence—the fall of sear leaves from a poplar is as fully ordained as the tumbling of an avalanche."[12]

The implications of such a view, rooted in biblical texts like Ephesians 1:11, Acts 17:28, Jeremiah 10:23, Proverbs 16:9, 20:24, etc., are staggering. History is not a record of merely random occurrences or even the cause and effect of human decisions, but ultimately the plan of God to glorify His Son and save for Himself a people. Whether your children are studying ancient Egypt, the Renaissance masters, or the Navajo Indians, it all comes back to this overarching plan.

Christian homeschoolers should place a special emphasis on *Church* history, since the story of redemption and the building of Christ's kingdom is the central plot of all history. As one Puritan writer said, this whole earth was created to be the workshop in which God would create, call, form, mold, and sanctify His Church. When this work is completed and the Church of Christ has been fully built, this carpenter's workshop will be burned down, and a new earth will be created to be the permanent dwelling place of God's people. All history is important, but any study of history that ignores the stories of God's people misses the main point.

Timelines

In our own home, my wife and I have found the value of teaching our sons a history timeline. We began this when they were very young, and review the timeline each school year so that they will have it for life. In our case, we have used the Classical Conversations® timeline that includes around 180 historical eras and events, moving chronologically from Creation to September 11th, 2001.

The benefits of teaching your children a historical timeline are numerous. Children are able to see the logical order of people and events, making connections between a particular event and those which came before and after. The timeline provides a mental framework into which our kids can place everything else they learn. Every leader, warrior, writer, and inventor can be placed on the timeline, often shedding light on what shaped them and their influence on future generations. Every war, natural disaster, momentous discovery, philosophical development, and political revolution is viewed in its historical context. A timeline also helps our children know their own place in history, and what has unfolded in God's great story to make their present lives possible. This historical knowledge can inform the way they look at current issues, help them avoid the mistakes of the past, and hopefully will give them greater understanding of why other cultures differ from our own. Ultimately, we are convinced that learning a historical timeline equips our children to better engage with others in this world for Christ's glory.

Christian Biography

Have you ever considered how much of the Bible is biography? Sometimes the best instruction we can receive comes to us through *example* – the good or bad examples of others. *"Now these things happened to them as an example, but they were written down for our instruction, on whom the end of the ages has come"* (1st Corinthians 10:11). Hebrews 11 is often called the "Hall of Faith", and exhorts us to remember those who have gone before as models of persevering faith. Our children are given higher views of God and greater reasons to love and trust Him as they see His faithfulness in the lives of those who have come before.

Good Christian biographies serve our children in at least nine ways. First, they show them that God can do great things through ordinary people. Second, they teach our children that even the godliest men and women were still sinners who found their greatness in depending on God's grace. Third, good biographies call our children to repentance, convicting them of their own wrong attitudes or behaviors as they see them mirrored in the lives of others. Fourth, they highlight the greatness of the breadth and depth of God's mercy towards all kinds of people. Fifth, these stories serve as testimonies to God's faithfulness to His promises. Sixth, they help guard our children against overly-triumphalistic views of the Christian life. Seventh, Christian biographies remind our children that our actions have consequences. Eighth, they prepare our children to live well and die well. Finally, good Christian biographies lead them to worship God for His work in the lives of others. I've provided a list of some of our favorite Christian biographies at the end of this chapter.

Expositing History

Surprising to some, the study of history can be very similar to the study of literature. In one sense, it is the study of the greatest novel that has ever been written. It is *God's* novel, His story, and every age is the unfolding of another chapter. You and I are characters within this story.

The Bible often presents history in terms of a *book*. In Revelation 5, God's plans for the earth are presented to John as being contained in a scroll with seven seals. Because a fully unrolled scroll could take up a great deal of space, it was common for them to have seals that held various sections of the scroll together. To unroll a particular section of the scroll, you would need to break its seal.

The question arises: *"Who is worthy to open the scroll and break its seals?"* (Revelation 5:2). The apostle begins to weep, because no one is found worthy to open the scroll. God's glorious plans will be left unfulfilled. Then, one of the elders says to John, *"Weep no more; behold, the Lion of the tribe of Judah, the Root of David, has conquered, so that he can open the scroll and its seven seals."* (Revelation 5:5). Thus, the Bible sees history as a book written by God, and brought to fruition through the authority of Jesus Christ, His Son.

Yet it is not just world history that is presented as a book in the pages of the Bible. Our own personal histories are presented the same way. On the Day of Judgment, we are told that all people great and small will stand before the throne, and that *books* will be opened. These books, different from the Lamb's Book of Life, are the record of our every thought, word, and deed. They contain our *individual* histories. Moreover, David says in the Psalms: *"Your eyes saw my unformed substance; **in your book** were written, every one of them, the days that were formed for me, when as yet there was none of them"* (Psalm 139:16, emphasis added). For David, his whole life had already been written by God in a book before his conception.

Once we have begun to see history as *His Story*, God's great book, it makes sense that our God Grids for history will have much in common with those we have created in our study of literature. The key difference is that this novel is *the* Novel, written by *the* Author, and is entirely true.

So how might we exposit this great novel to see more of God's glory? First, we can select any person or event in history. Then we might ask: What is one lesson God is teaching through that person's life or that event? From there, we can proceed just as we did with our literature God Grid.

However, I must offer up one warning. It is important that we always test the lesson we draw from a historical person or event against the teaching of Scripture. We are fallen people, and we are prone to draw *false* lessons. For example, suppose your children were learning about a man who bought a $5 lottery ticket and won ten million dollars. They might deduce the lesson that God blesses those who gamble. But of course, that would be a *false* lesson. Proverbs 13:11 says that *"Wealth gained hastily will dwindle."* To help us learn the right lessons, we should always approach the study of history through the lens of a biblical worldview.

From God

For the purposes of example, let us consider the story of the first English settlement in the New World: Jamestown. The account of these first English settlers on American soil is a fascinating one, and certainly a story we will want our children to learn. Along the way, they will read about "The Starving Time", the winter of 1609-1610 when almost three-fourths of the colonists died of starvation and disease. When one considers the plights of those desperate people, it is rather astounding that they did not demand to be taken back to England on the next arriving ship, but instead persevered through many harrowing trials to establish England's first colony: Virginia. One lesson we might learn from their story is this: It is often through perseverance that great accomplishments are achieved.

Now, before we move into our God Grid, we must make sure our lesson is true. Is there solid Scriptural ground supporting this lesson? There is. One verse that immediately comes to mind is Galatians 6:9: *"And let us not grow weary of doing good, for in due season we will reap, if we do not give up."*

What are some facts about the truth that it is often through perseverance that great accomplishments are achieved? Our children might mention that perseverance can be difficult. They might suggest that great accomplishments take time. You might even point out that there are few accomplishments that could be considered "great" that are also easy. Often, part of what makes an accomplishment great is the obstacles that were overcome to reach it. My son Jonathan pointed out that our world would be quite boring if everything was easy.

What does this truth teach us about God? It teaches us that God delights to bless those who have persevered for a good cause. He has not called His people to be quitters, but people of commitment to that which is good and right. Moreover, He is our ultimate example, persevering in His faithfulness throughout all generations. Jesus Christ came as a true Man, and His obedience to His Father was *hard*. He faced many trials and was tempted in many ways to give up His divine mission. Yet throughout His life Jesus persevered in doing right, even when it meant death on a cross. The result was that His Father gave Him all authority in Heaven and on earth, and exalted Him above every name. Hebrews 12:1-2 says,

*Therefore, since we are surrounded by so great a cloud of witnesses, let us also lay aside every weight, and sin which clings so closely, and let us **run with endurance** the race that is set before us, looking to Jesus, the founder and perfecter of our faith, **who for the joy that was set before him endured the cross, despising the shame, and is seated at the right hand of the throne of God** (emphasis added).*

Here is our ultimate example of perseverance: the Lord Jesus Christ.

Through God
What role does this truth play in Scripture? There are many wonderful examples of perseverance in the Bible that our children might recall. Benjamin (my eight-year-old) thought first of Shadrach, Meshach, and Abednego, who remained steadfastly obedient to God even when threatened with fire. Jeremiah continued to deliver God's message though his life was threatened, he was put in stocks, he was cast into a pit, and the people refused to listen to him. The persistent widow in Luke 18 continued to pester the judge until he finally relented and gave into her request. The apostle Paul remained faithful to his missionary calling though he was imprisoned, shipwrecked, beaten, and stoned. Though his hardships lasted many days, faithful Job refused to curse God, but endured the trials God sent to Him. *"You have heard of the steadfastness of Job, and you have seen the purpose of the Lord, how the Lord is compassionate and merciful"* (James 5:11).

Where do we see perseverance leading to great accomplishments in history? The examples are more than we could name! Thomas Edison persevered through over a thousand failures before he finally succeeded in inventing a working lightbulb. Henry Ford had five business ventures fail before founding the Ford Motor Company. The author Jack London submitted his first story to publishers over six hundred times before one finally accepted it. Many wounded soldiers have been remarkable examples of perseverance, enduring painful rehabilitation and ultimately accomplishing recoveries and feats thought impossible for men or women with their injuries. These kinds of discussions inspire and encourage our children, and by God's grace can have a lifelong impact on their character.

For God
Does this truth have an eternal purpose? It depends on how we look at it. On the one hand, heaven will be a place of perfection. Persevering in worship and service to our God will be easy, because the obstacles that come through sin will have been removed. Many of the challenges that face us here and now will no longer exist.

On the other hand, perseverance does have an eternal purpose because it is only *through* perseverance in faith that we will enter Heaven. This is the message of Jesus' parable of the four soils. As Jesus stated on multiple occasions, *"the one who endures to the end will be saved"* (Matthew 10:22; 24:13; Mark 13:13). Hebrews 3:14 says it this way: *"For we have come to share in Christ, if indeed we hold our original confidence firm to the end."*

Finally, how can we glorify God through this truth? One answer is that when we persevere through obstacles *for God's sake*, in obedience to Him, we show to the world how much He is worth to us. God's value and greatness is often best seen in the perseverance of His people's faith and obedience through trials. Christians ought to be *known* for their persevering character, which is why people used to talk about the "Protestant work ethic." In a discussion like this, we have a valuable opportunity to challenge our children to honor God by persevering in doing good even when it is hard. One homeschool mom told me recently that she repeats the same answer when her children complain that some assignment or chore is hard: "We *do* hard in this family." We as Christian parents want to teach our children not to run away from difficulty, but to persevere through it that great things might be accomplished for Christ.

Helps for God-Centered History
I mentioned earlier in this chapter that our family enjoys Christian biography. Here are some of our favorite series of biographies for kids, plus one single biography at the end that happens to be my all-time favorite:

- The *Lightkeepers* by Irene Howat, often referred to as the *Ten Boys* and *Ten Girls* books
- The *Trail Blazers* series by Derick Bingham
- The *Christian Heroes: Then and Now* series by Janet and Geoff Benge, published by YWAM
- The *Bitesize Biographies* series by multiple authors, published by Evangelical Press
- The *Building on the Rock* series by Joel R. Beeke and Diana Kleyn
- *King of the Cannibals: The Story of John G. Paton, Missionary to the Hebrides* by Jim Cromarty
- *Trial and Triumph: Stories from Church History* by Richard M. Hannula

The God Grid

(Sample from homeschool students[4])

*"For from him and through him and to him are all things.
To him be glory forever. Amen."*
- Romans 11:36

THE WATERGATE SCANDAL

TRUTH: Deception will always have Consequences.
Scriptural Support: Proverbs 19:9

From God (Origin)
1. What are some facts about this truth?

- Deception is the act of deceiving others.
- Deception is wrong.
- Consequences are necessary
- Consequences can often be painful.

2. What does this truth teach us about God?

- God wants us to do what is right.
- God knows what is best for us.
- God is willing to punish us for the sin of deception.
- God Himself will never deceive.

Through God (Providence)
3. What role does this truth play in Scripture?

- David deceived others and bore the consequence of his son's death.
- The devil is called a deceiver.
- Jesus said that the Antichrist will deceive, and will one day be thrown into hell.

4. What role does this truth play in history?

- Richard Nixon tried to deceive America, and bore the consequence of having to resign and having his public image destroyed.
- Many families have suffered greatly because of deception in the home.

For God (Purpose)
5. Does this truth have an eternal purpose?

- In some circumstances, the consequences of deception are not greatly experienced in this life, but will come to fruition in the Day of Judgment. The consequences of deception may be eternal or both eternal *and* temporal, but never just temporal.

6. How might we use this truth to further glorify God?

- We should warn ourselves and others about the consequences of deception, that we would be honest people who trust God.
- We should thank God that He is sovereign even over acts of deception, so that He is able to work even those acts for the good of His people and the glory of His Name.

The God Grid
(Use this blank grid to give it a try yourself!)

*"For from him and through him and to him are all things.
To him be glory forever. Amen."*
- Romans 11:36

WORLD WAR II

TRUTH: _____

SCRIPTURAL SUPPORT: _____

From God (Origin)
1. What are some facts about this truth?

_____
_____
_____
_____
_____

2. What does this truth teach us about God?

_____
_____
_____
_____
_____

Through God (Providence)
3. What role does this truth play in Scripture?

_____
_____
_____
_____
_____

4. What role does this truth play in history?

_____
_____
_____
_____
_____

For God (Purpose)
5. Does this truth have an eternal purpose?

_____
_____
_____
_____
_____

6. How might we use this truth to further glorify God?

_____
_____
_____
_____
_____

8)

A Parting Word

---

*"May you be strengthened with all power,
according to his glorious might,
for all endurance and patience with joy."*
- Colossians 1:11

The central impulse of this book has been to encourage you in helping your children see the glory of God in every subject. There are many more subjects we could talk about, and from time to time I will speak to those other subjects on the blog associated with this book (godcenteredhomeschool.com). Many of the principles and ideas we have discussed can be transferred to other subjects of study not dealt with directly.

Using Romans 11:36 as a grid is only *one* way to point your children to God in their studies. God Grids are only *one* way of using Romans 11:36. In other words, we have only scratched the surface of possibilities, and I hope you and your family will embark on the grand adventure of finding other methods to see Him everywhere. As for God Grids, they belong to you, and can be reimagined in many ways. For younger children, there may be ways to ask the questions in more specific ways to help them take their first steps in learning the art of making connections. For older children, many more questions could be added to further unpack how the subject of study relates to God in terms of origin, providence, and purpose. Feel free to adjust the grid, rewrite the questions, and reimagine the possible uses in order to best fit your family. If I've stirred up your thinking at all towards more practical ways to lead your children into worship during the homeschool day, I am satisfied.

Allow me to close this book with a prayer of blessing for you and your family:

Father, thank You for loving us so deeply. Thank You for Christ, Your glorious Son, and the salvation we have in Him. Thank You also for our children, and the joyful stewardship You have entrusted to us.

I ask that You would pour out Your blessings upon the family of this reader. Give them an eagle-eye for Your glory, and satisfy their souls with Your character and works. Bless the children, and cause them to grow in knowledge, understanding, and wisdom. Most of all, save them and make them Your servants. Equip them to find their happiness in being fruitful followers of Christ in this world.

I ask that You will give grace to the parents. May their marriage be strong, their devotion to you ever-growing, and their growth in patience and love swift. Be the Treasure of their hearts, and may they share this Treasure with their children as they homeschool.

Father, we commit ourselves and our families to You afresh. Glorify Your Name in us.

In Jesus' Name, Amen.

Notes

[1]This last statement deserves a closer look. After all, the Scriptures do tell us to be happy. *"Rejoice in the Lord always; again I will say, rejoice"* (Philippians 4:4, cf. 1 Thessalonians 5:16). We are also told that joy is a fruit of the Spirit. It places second in the famous list of Galatians 5:22-23, second only to love, with which joy is so intimately connected. As a fruit of the Spirit, we recognize that our joy is ultimately a gift to us from God, an attribute of His granted to us and cultivated in us by His hand (like all the others in the list). Our God is a happy God (1 Timothy 1:11), and the joy that we are commanded to pursue is joy *in the Lord*. Our joy is connected to the joy that Christ has as the Son of God, and in our union with Him His joy becomes ours as we appropriate it through faith. So in a very real way, the command to rejoice in the Lord is a command to be happy as Christ is happy, and therefore as God is happy.

[2]I highly recommend Piper's book *Desiring God* for a thoroughly biblical defense of this proposition.

[3]Quoted in *Life and Works of Rev. Charles H. Spurgeon* by Henry Davenport Northrop,1892. p.525.

[4]The sample God Grids in this book were partially taken from those produced by a special group of homeschool students that I had the privilege of tutoring in our local Classical Conversations® Challenge 1 program. They were all 14 or 15 at the time of this writing. A big shout out to Reagan B., Josiah C., Anna D., Thomas M., Adele S., Benjamin S., and Ben S.

[5]For the following discussion, I am especially indebted to Vern Poythress and James Nickel, whose books first drew my attention to the attributes of God in a basic equation. Poythress' book is called *Redeeming Mathematics: A God-Centered Approach.* Nickel's book is called *Mathematics: Is God Silent?* The order of my discussion here follows closely the order of Poythress.

[6]We used a simple, specific equation in this chapter for the sake of introducing the skill, but there are many specific equations that would make it harder for our children to make connections, especially to Scripture and history. If I asked my sons to use the God Grid on the equation 177 x 103 = 18,231, for example, specific connections would be harder to come by. If I instead ask them to use the God Grid on the operation of multiplication, or on the concept of an equation, or even on the concept of numbers, they will have much more to work with and the grid will likely prove more rewarding.

[7]*Redeeming Science: A God-Centered Approach*. Vern Poythress, (2006, Crossway Publishing), pp.26-27.

[8]*War of Words: Getting to the Heart of Your Communication Struggles*. Paul David Tripp, (2000, P&R Publishing), p.8.

[9]*God's Way of Reconciliation: An Exposition of Ephesians*. D. Martyn Lloyd-Jones, (2003, Baker Books), p.69.

[10] *The Sign of the Beaver*. Elizabeth George Speare, (1983, Yearling Books), pp. 116-117.

[11] *To Kill a Mockingbird*. Harper Lee, (1960, Grand Central Publishing), p. 283

[12]*Sermons of the Rev. C. H. Spurgeon of London* by Charles H. Spurgeon, 1857. p.201.

A special thank you to Melissa Pryer and Crystal Nale for reading the manuscript and offering many helpful suggestions and corrections. This book is much better because of you.

Justin Nale is pastor of Mount Hermon Missionary Baptist Church in Rocky Mount, NC. He and his wife Crystal have been actively involved in homeschooling their two sons and seeking to serve other homeschoolers for more than a decade.

To contact Justin about speaking at your event or for other inquiries, please use this email address:

justin@godcenteredhomeschool.com

Made in the USA
Las Vegas, NV
12 April 2023

70509115R00075